INSIGHT

Vanc...

APA PUBLICATIONS
Part of the Langenscheidt Publishing Group

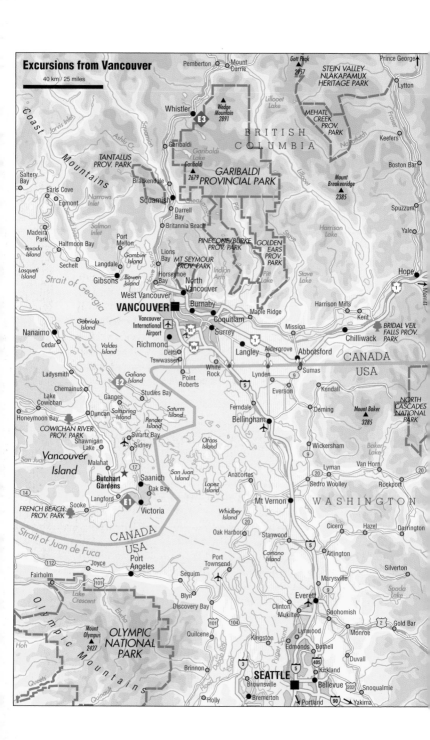

Excursions from Vancouver

40 km / 25 miles

Welcome

This guidebook combines the interests and enthusiasms of two of the world's best-known information providers: Insight Guides, who have set the standard for visual travel guides since 1970, and Discovery Channel, the world's premier source of non-fiction television programming. Its aim is to show readers the best of Vancouver in a series of itineraries originally devised by Joel W Rogers and later enhanced and reconstructed by Pat Kramer.

There can be few cities in the world that are so urbane yet so cradled in wilderness as Vancouver, where mountain peaks loom high above grand boulevards and there are sudden sunlit glimpses of sunlit water glistening between skyscrapers. It is a youthful city, built and shaped by new arrivals, which has become a place of innovation yet still guided by its pioneer spirit.

All of this is reflected in Vancouver's unconventional architecture, its historic downtown district, its ethnic neighbourhoods, its internationally renowned cuisine, its wealth of outdoor activities and its considerable number of museums. The 10 carefully-planned itineraries in this guide will help any visitor to discover and appreciate the varied aspects of the city. They are followed by three excursions to the surrounding area, the picturesque streets of Victoria, the idyllic Gulf Islands and to Whistler resort, with its year-round sporting activities.

Pat Kramer is the author of several guidebooks on topics such as First Nations culture in Alaska and gardens of British Columbia. The British Columbia writer, who also takes photographs, is very familiar with the region, so much so that she is a tour director and guest lecturer on cruise ships, providing entertaining talks about nature.

Kramer built on the original edition, which was produced by writer Joel W Rogers, who enjoyed visiting British Columbia so much that he eventually moved to an area of Vancouver called Kitsilano, across English Bay from the West End. He was an enthusiastic resident of that particular neighbourhood when he wrote his manuscript.

Pages 2/3: Downtown and the mountains

Pages 8/9: An ancient tree dominates the forest

History & *Culture*

aptain George Vancouver pacing the quarterdeck as a group of natives approached in cedar canoes is a romantic beginning for a city. But the arrival of His Majesty's ships for one day in 1792 – embellished to form a boaster's tale of intrepid mariners, fur trappers and gold prospectors – is not where this history begins. The origins and currents of this city run perhaps 10,000, or even 12,000 years deeper. The land that now supports a diverse population of more than 2 million has long been home to bands of First Nations tribes, known collectively as the Northwest Coast people, who may have arrived by land bridge from Asia, island hopping along the Aleutians, migrating south both along the coast and down ice-free corridors, to settle in the delta and inlet of an enormous river. In this place, where millions of silvery salmon swam for seven months of each year, the great city of Vancouver would grow.

The People of the Grass

Throughout the broken and intricate fjords to the north and the broad-beached alluvial plains to the south, the people built their villages. Free from the ever-present threat of scarcity that plagued the natives of the plains and prairies, and untroubled by the very harsh winters that prevail just about everywhere else in the country, the Coast nations had time to create their art and their stories. This led to the development of what some modern-day anthropologists consider the richest culture of all the hunter-gathering peoples of the world – including the making of magnificent totem poles and other forms of decorative wood carving.

Speaking variations of a language known as Coast Salish, the ancestors of the Squamish, Burrard, Tsleil-Waututh, Musqueam (Xw'muthk'i'um), Tsawwassen, Coquitlam (Kwayhquitlam), Katzie and Semiahmoo bands shared the land that is now known as Vancouver. North Vancouver's Burrard band claim descent from a separate Halkomelem-speaking nation, the Tsleil'waututh. The Musqueam, 'the people of the grass', built their villages along the salt-grass margins of the Fraser River delta. The Squamish lived on the north shores of Burrard Inlet and in their northern winter villages at the windy head of Howe Sound, giving them their name, 'strong winds'. The Kwantlen established villages near present-day New Westminster, and the Tsawwassen lived to the south in Delta and Richmond.

By all accounts these bands lived in relative harmony with their neighbours, moving annually between summer camps and winter villages, and holding lavish entertainments, known as *potlatches*. Important local ceremonies involved dancers wearing cedar-bark costumes and a plumed, bug-eyed skhwaykhwey mask.

Left: the son of a Tsimshian totem carver, of the Northwest Coast tribes
Right: carved out of history

It may have been a Musqueam band which in 1791 welcomed the Spanish explorer Don José Maria Narvaez, as his 11-m (36-ft) schooner stood off Point Grey. A year later a British man, Captain George Vancouver (1757–1798), on his epic voyage in search of the Northwest Passage would sail the ship *Discovery* through the First Narrows and into history.

Between 1792, when Captain Vancouver charted Burrard Inlet, and 1851, when placer gold (deposits in sand and gravel) was discovered on the Fraser, British Columbia became a crown colony. The power and population of local First Nations dwindled with the establishment of the Hudson's Bay Company's Fort Langley fur trading post and the administrative centre of New Westminster up the Fraser River. By 1862, epidemics had wiped out two-thirds (around 80,000) of the British Columbia bands. The remainder were excluded and awarded no rights or power in the new province.

The Finest Trees in the World

It wasn't gold that brought settlers to British Columbia, however, it was timber. George Vancouver noted in his log, 'Well covered with trees of large growth principally of the pine tribe'. Firs as high as contemporary Vancouver's tallest buildings were perfect for the masts of Royal Navy ships and in the 1860s a number of reserves around Burrard Inlet met the demand. By 1865 Vancouver's first sawmill, Stamp's Mill, was thriving. Living in the perpetual shade of fir, hemlock, spruce and cedar, the settlers chopped out clearings and learned to girdle and to burn the massive trees until they fell. Loggers fed the mills, and the entire region became a haze of slash burning as the virgin rainforest was steadily cut.

By 1870 the Vancouver-to-be was an 11-hectare (28-acre), two-block settlement with a population of 50. The locals named it Gastown after the loquacious and frequently inebriated 'Gassy' Jack Deighton, proprietor of the city's first 'watering hole', where gold miners mixed with ships' hands and loggers. Many spoke Chinook, a native trade language, in part because the newcomers were Russian, Chilean, Kanakan (Hawaiian), Portuguese, Belgian, French, Spanish, Finnish, Austrian and American.

In 1884 Gastown was renamed Granville, then changed its name to Vancouver at the suggestion of William Van Horne, the general manager of the

Canadian Pacific Railway. It was not only the name that changed. More than 500 buildings rose in anticipation of the new railhead. Thousands laboured, property repeatedly changed hands, dirt streets were extended and the forests razed, until the afternoon of 13 June 1886 – when it all burned down. In one hour, an out-of-control slash fire swept through the streets, forcing people into Burrard Inlet and False Creek. But within a year the city was rebuilt, this time with brick, and on 23 May 1887, the eve of Queen Victoria's birthday, the first transcontinental train arrived.

The Train to the Future

With the arrival of the railway, the future of the region began to take shape. Vancouver was already destined to be Canada's western port city, the only place with both a route through British Columbia's mountains and a deep-water harbour. Dubbed the most beautiful steamships the world has ever seen, the Canadian Pacific's Empresses began shipping raw silk and tea across the North Pacific. These goods were quickly loaded onto the cross-country railway for re-export to England and beyond. As Canada's Pacific Rim trade came of age, the area and the company began to grow rich.

Vancouver benefited greatly from the reign of the Canadian Pacific Railway, as this Montréal-based company orchestrated amenities a frontier city could never command. In 1891 the city's first tram-based public transit system, the Interurban, began to operate. Sand was added to English Bay Beach and a very large rock was imported to shield men and women bathers, permitting them to change in privacy. Vancouver was also fortunate in having a population that hailed from every corner of the world, sowing the seeds of today's uniquely cosmopolitan city.

A City of Immigrants

The cultural mix was not achieved without some pain. Chinese, Japanese and East Indian immigrants, along with the First Nations, were all persecuted throughout the early history of the city. Arriving in 1858 from California and Hong Kong, about 5,000 Chinese came to prospect for gold in the interior's Cariboo gold fields, then from 1881 to 1885 a second wave of 17,000 Chinese, mainly from Canton, arrived to work on the railway. They went on to labour in the coastal canneries and to serve in the kitchens of almost every substantial house from Victoria to Vancouver. Alarmed by the surging

Left: felling the giants
Above: Haida Indians **Right:** new arrivals

populations of 'orientals', the province and the federal government passed the Chinese Immigration Act of 1885, the first of many laws that would deny Asians the right to vote, to lease crown land or to choose their professions.

The Japanese began arriving in numbers after 1896. They pioneered the herring fisheries and exported dog salmon to Japan. They worked the mills and farms, and opened shops around the 200 block of Powell Street.

During the 1880s, many indigenous people perished. Torn between their ancient ways of seasonal food gathering and the new-found wealth at the mills and canneries, the fabric of their lives began to unravel. Relegated in some cases to reservations, their concept of territory, family fish camps and sacred sites was superseded by European ownership. Christian missions began operating residential schools, and aboriginal children were seized from their families by law and forced into programmes of 'civilization.'

A Coming of Age

At the turn of the 20th century Vancouver began the greatest growth period of its history. It had already become the financial, transportation and supply centre of British Columbia. Now mining expanded into copper, lead and zinc; coal remained number one, and gold production tripled. There were 49 salmon canneries on the Fraser. Wheat farmers on the prairies swallowed up 75 percent of British Columbia's lumber production, and the new market for pulp and paper created 100 new forestry companies in 10 years.

Between 1910 and 1912 the city's population quadrupled from 27,000 to 122,000 and its limits grew from 4sq. km (1½sq. miles) to 35sq. km (13½sq. miles). Grand buildings rose to shadow Gastown: the Dominion Trust soared to 13 storeys in 1909, but was quickly topped by newspaper publisher Louis B Taylor's 17-storey Sun-World Tower. Cars began to appear, but streetcars carried most people to work, on 400km (250 miles) of track. Canada's first artificial ice rink, the Arena, opened – the largest indoor rink in the

Above: Vancouver c1930

world and home to the Vancouver Millionaires, the city's first hockey team. In 1915 they won the Western hockey championship. New neighbourhoods began to take shape as immigrants moved into Strathcona, Grandview and East Hastings, office workers built in Kitsilano and Dunbar, and socialites moved into Point Grey, Kerrisdale and Shaughnessy Heights.

Vancouver's natural beaches – English Bay, Kitsilano, Jericho and Spanish Banks – were purchased and the University of British Columbia was sited at Point Grey. At that time 72 percent of Vancouver's business magnates had only a high school education. In 1912 Mary Henrietta McNaughton was elected to the school board, the first woman to gain office in the city.

When World War I began in 1914, 28,000 citizens enlisted, the highest proportion from a single North American city to go to the trenches. They included 200 Japanese-Canadian volunteers, of whom 54 were killed and 92 wounded. By the end of the war Vancouver was a city of wage earners. And though the economy cooled, the town matured, becoming the first Canadian city to adopt comprehensive zoning laws, while new commercial strips followed the trolley tracks into the suburbs. More parks and six golf courses came into being, and there was skiing at Grouse Mountain. In 1920 the city's population turned out in droves to watch the famous illusionist Houdini suspend himself in a strait jacket from the top of the Sun Tower. The area was beginning to play. But then the Depression hit.

Depression and Recovery

Dependent upon export-based industries, Vancouver reeled from layoffs and bankruptcies. Thirty percent of the population was out of work in 1936, and the city foreclosed on 31,000 properties for non-payment of taxes. North Vancouver and Burnaby went bankrupt. The only bright spot was the Irish Guinness family's investment in the Lions Gate, a landmark suspension bridge that opened in 1938 to service their property developments on the North Shore. It would take a war to return to prosperity.

Despite their citizenship, military service and losses in World War I, the World War II years began with the internment of Japanese citizens – 9,000 in Vancouver alone – and their property auctioned at roughly ten cents on the dollar. At the same time, skilled immigrants who had been relegated to farm labour in peace time became crucial to the retooling for war. Women went to work as never before, 60,000 strong in the city's shipyards, mills and businesses.

The Post-War Years

After the war, Vancouver experienced explosive growth. The suburbs doubled in population, and the flavour of the city began to blend into an international stew as refugees from Europe and Asia flooded in. The street car era ended just as Vancouver began to feel big-city pressures. Crowds and traffic were increasing, with no solution in sight. The West End was entirely re-zoned for

Right: Japanese internment

high-rise apartments; plans were afoot for the 'urban renewal' of Chinatown and Strathcona. In 1967 plans for the first of 14 freeways were unveiled, but community protest and high costs caused the planners to retreat and Vancouver remains the only major North American city without a freeway.

By 1970 the influx of immigrants had turned many neighbourhoods into celebrated ethnic communities, with 10,000 Italian-born residents around Commercial Street, Greeks on Fourth, 8,000 Germans calling Robson Street 'Robsonstrasse', and Chinatown enriched by the influx of 15,000 people from Hong Kong and Taiwan. Almost everyone could unite in cheers as the Vancouver Canucks played their first game in the National Hockey League.

The Saltwater City

In 1983 BC Place opened as the world's largest air-supported stadium, and three years later Expo '86, a World Exposition, celebrated Vancouver's 100th birthday, thrusting the region into the international limelight. It funded the light-rail 'SkyTrain' and landmark Canada Place, but the most profound and lasting effect was the raising of the Pacific Northwest's image on the international horizon. In the wake of Expo '86, Hong Kong multi-billionaire Li Ka-shing purchased the entire 83-hectare (204-acre) site for $125 million, causing the world's financial community to take notice. Today Li Ka-shing's highrise condominiums continue to spring up, while the traditional single-family home is an endangered species, due to spiralling costs.

During the 1990s, a flurry of new construction included the innovative Vancouver Public Library building, General Motors Place stadium – nicknamed 'The Garage' – for hockey, basketball and concerts, and the spiffy Centre in Vancouver for Performing Arts (formerly the Ford Centre). Strangely, throughout this period, Vancouver's buildings and alleyways began to masquerade as other cities – New York, Chicago, Seattle or even London. Each year more than 200 movie and television productions are filmed here and celebrity spotting is commonplace in 'Hollywood North'.

Vancouver is consistently hailed as one of the best cities in the world in which to live, and its proximity to the acclaimed ski resort of Whistler is a definite bonus. On 1 July 2003 – Canada Day – the International Olympic Committee selected Vancouver to host the 2010 Winter Olympics and Paralympic Games; the city partied for days.

While the financial future of the region appears secure and the world increasingly notices this lively and magnificently scenic enclave by the sea, it is the people, not the financiers, who have made 'Saltwater City' what it is today. Still noted as the city that gave birth to Greenpeace, Vancouver prides itself on its environmental awareness and the quality of life that it maintains for its diverse mixture of citizens.

Left: environmentalists protest

History Highlights

Circa 8000BC Earliest findings of the Northwest Coast people settling along the shores of the Fraser River.

500BC Earliest date of inhabitation within Vancouver proper at Ee'yull-mough Village, Jericho Beach.

AD1791 Spanish navigator José Maria Navárez enters Burrard Inlet.

1792 Captain George Vancouver claims the region for Great Britain.

1827 Fort Langley, a Hudson's Bay Company fur trading post, is built on the south shore of the Fraser River.

1850 British Columbia's First Nations population drops from an estimated 150,000 in the 1770s to 60,000, due largely to smallpox.

1851 Gold discovered on the Fraser drainage brings 22,000 prospectors, including the first Chinese residents. Great Britain proclaims the territory the 'Colony of British Columbia'.

1864 The first timber export, 277,500 board feet of fir, is loaded aboard the barque *Ellen Lewis* bound for Adelaide, Australia. Governor Douglas creates First Nations reservations.

1867 Jack Deighton builds a saloon that becomes the centre of 'Gastown'.

1872 The provincial government amends the Voter Act to exclude Chinese and native residents.

1884 Floating salmon-cannery refuse is blamed for fish die-off in Coal Harbour: Vancouver's first pollution alert.

1886 The city's 1,000 buildings burn to the ground in an hour and are rebuilt within one year. 'Gastown' is renamed Granville, then becomes the City of Vancouver. Lauchlan Hamilton, the Canadian Pacific Railway's civil engineer, proposes Stanley Park.

1887 The first CPR transcontinental rail and steamship service is joined in Vancouver, linking the Orient to Europe in 29 days.

1890s The first golf course west of the Mississippi is laid out at Jericho; the first suburb, Mount Pleasant, is planned.

1914–18 Vancouver sends a higher proportion of soldiers to the French front than any other North American city.

1920s Wreck Beach becomes known for its clothing-optional bathing.

1929 British Columbia has 4,000 logging operations and 350 mills.

1937 Strathcona Elementary School teaches students who represent 57 nationalities.

1947–48 Asian and First Nations residents granted the vote in provincial, and later national, elections.

1952 Diners can now have a drink with their food.

1967 Vancouverites found the environmental group Greenpeace.

1974 Eight forestry companies have control of 82 percent of British Columbia's harvesting rights.

1978 An estimated 50 percent of the city's prime office and apartment buildings are owned by Hong Kong interests.

1986 Expo '86 draws 22 million visitors and establishes Vancouver as an international tourist and trade destination.

1992 Vancouver-born Kim Campbell becomes British Columbia's first Prime Minister of Canada.

1993 Average detached house price in Vancouver reaches $500,000; in the region it is $350,000.

1999 The population of Vancouver approaches 2 million, about 35 percent of whom are Asian in origin.

2002 The Economist Intelligence Unit survey hails Vancouver (tied with Melbourne, Australia) as the top city to live.

2003 Vancouver is selected to host the 2010 Olympic and Paralympic Winter Games.

2004 Work begins on Olympic venues. Property prices boom again.

history/culture

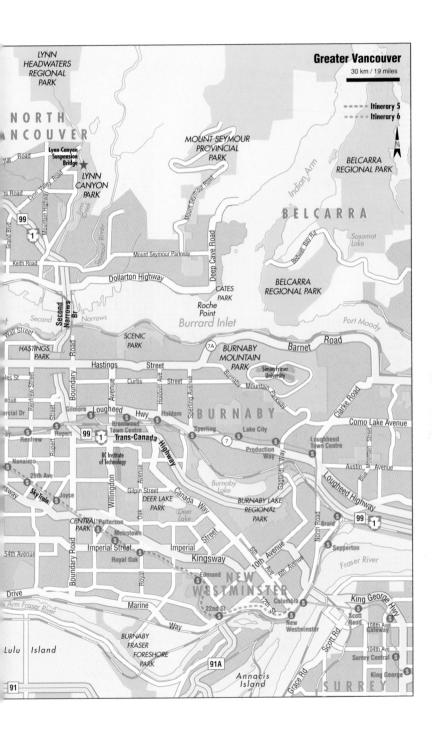

Orientation

Vancouver is widely acknowledged by those lucky enough to have done the comparisons, to be among the three most beautiful cities in the world and one of the best places in which to live. Not only does it have wonderful scenery, with water on three sides and spectacular mountains rising nearby, it has a vibrant arts scene and plenty of outdoor activities. It also has a population who have developed a unique character. Just as Toronto has become the 'New York of Canada', Vancouver has become a more northerly, less extreme California, with a mix of laid-back attitude and vigorous health-conscious lifestyle.

It's very easy for visitors to get around this lovely city. With water on three sides of the downtown area, it has all been carefully contained, and the lack of main highways within the city proper makes walking a pleasure. There's a sizeable downtown population, too, who regularly take to the streets on foot, to shop during the day and to enjoy the vibrant atmosphere on warm summer evenings. This, adds greatly to the character of this lovely place. And, as if it needed anything more, Vancouver is situated in the only Canadian province where the average winter temperature is consistently above freezing point.

The areas of the city that you will want to explore are eminently walk-able, and they are all linked by an excellent integrated system of public transport, comprising the elevated SkyTrain, which has fine views, buses, the West Coast Express trains, and the ferries that head out across the water in all directions. For trips further afield there are airplanes. What small gaps there might be in this network are amply filled by the city's taxis. Several of the itineraries included in this guide explore the chunk of land that juts out into Burrard Inlet, including the modern downtown area, historic Gastown, beautiful Stanley Park, Granville Island and colourful Chinatown.

There are lots of water-borne trips to choose from too, including a jour-ney on the Aquabus that takes you to Kitsilano Beach in Itinerary 8, a spot of sea kayaking for Itinerary 9, the SeaBus to the North Shore in Itinerary 10, and ferries to Vancouver Island and the Gulf Islands (which you may also reach via a short, but scenic flight by floatplane).

Most of the tours described in this book can be done quite easily without a car, but you might want to rent a vehicle for Itinerary 5, to enable you to take in both of the fine walks we have devised for you. You will definitely need a car for the excursions to the Gulf Islands and to Whistler. Although the latter is served by public transport, it's much more fun to make the two-hour drive indepen-dently, so that you can fully enjoy the beauty of the Sea-to-Sky Highway and stop to explore or just drink in the views whenever you feel like it along the way.

Left: Vancouver's changing skyline
Right: hop on a trolley

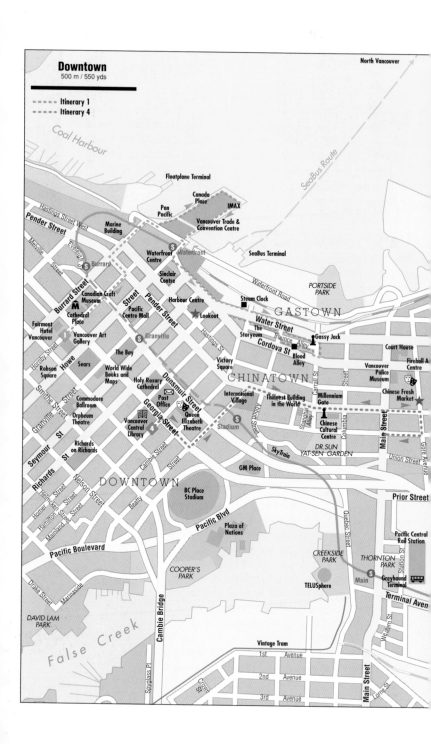

Downtown
500 m / 550 yds

- - - - Itinerary 1
- - - - Itinerary 4

North Vancouver

Coal Harbour

Floatplane Terminal

Canada Place

Pan Pacific

IMAX

Vancouver Trade & Convention Centre

SeaBus Route

Hastings Street West

Pender Street

Marine Building

Waterfront Centre

Waterfront

SeaBus Terminal

Melville

Street

Burrard

Sinclair Centre

Waterfront Road

PORTSIDE PARK

Street

Canadian Craft Museum

Harbour Centre

Steam Clock

GASTOWN

Burrard Street

Pender Street

Pacific Centre Mall

Lookout

Water Street

The Storyeum

Cordova St

Gassy Jack

Court House

Cathedral Place

Fairmont Hotel Vancouver

Vancouver Art Gallery

Granville

Trounce Alley

Blood Alley

Firehall A Centre

Vancouver Police Museum

Hornby Street

Robson Square

Howe

Sears

The Bay

Hastings St.

Victory Square

CHINATOWN

Chinese Fresh Market

Smithe Street

Granville

St.

World Wide Books and Maps

Holy Rosary Cathedral

Dunsmuir Street

International Village

Thinnest Building in the World

Millennium Gate

Carrall St.

Street

Commodore Ballroom

Post Office

Abbott Street

Chinese Cultural Centre

Shanghai Alley

Columbia

Orpheum Theatre

Georgia Street

Queen Elizabeth Theatre

Stadium

Main Street

Seymour

St.

Vancouver Central Library

SkyTrain

DR. SUN YAT-SEN GARDEN

Richards on Richards

Cambie Street

GM Place

Union Street

Richards

Nelson Street

DOWNTOWN

BC Place Stadium

Prior Street

Henlocken Street

Homer Street

Hamilton Street

Mainland Street

Beatty

Pacific Blvd

Plaza of Nations

Quebec Street

Pacific Central Rail Station

THORNTON PARK

Station St.

Pacific Boulevard

COOPER'S PARK

CREEKSIDE PARK

Main

Greyhound Terminal

Drake Street

Marinaside

DAVID LAM PARK

TELUSphere

Terminal Aven

W Adam St.

Cambie Bridge

Spyglass Pl.

False Creek

Vintage Tram

1st Avenue

2nd Avenue

Crowe St.

3rd Avenue

Main Street

Lorne St.

city itineraries

1. THE HEART OF THE CITY *(see map, p22)*

Take a leisurely walk through the heart of Vancouver and let the pace and the people introduce you to a city where business, history, culture and cuisine all converge in the urban forest. This itinerary includes innovative architecture, the Vancouver Art Gallery, the Canadian Craft Museum and Canada Place, with its luxury ocean liners, then takes you around historic Gastown.

Vancouver's downtown area is compact, the walking is easy and relatively short-distanced. Check the weather and bring sunglasses even when it looks like rain. Plan on breakfast along the way, and make dinner reservations as early as possible from the suggestions at the end of this itinerary.

The business, hotel and department-store district of Vancouver is bustling, healthy, clean and fun. It is smart and young, expensive and bohemian, with an eclectic yet polite populace who wait at the traffic lights and dote on pedestrians. It is as fascinating an urban centre as you'll ever experience.

Around Robson Square

Begin your day at **Robson Square**, a public plaza on Robson Street between Hornby and Howe streets. Three blocks long, it was designed by renowned architect Arthur C Erickson in modern geometric design, and houses both the provincial government offices and the Law Courts. As you emerge from the overarching dome beside the roof garden waterfall, walk south along the ramped grand staircase to the highest point. Then turn and look around at the surrounding signature architecture of Vancouver.

To the west **Cathedral Place** (925 West Georgia Street at Hornby Street), designed by Paul Merrick, compliments the copper-roofed chateau-style **Fairmont Hotel Vancouver** (900 West Georgia Street), built by the Canadian Pacific Railway (CPR)

Top: Robson Square
Right: street entertainment

in its heyday. To the east is, as one architect put it, the 'ghastly' Sears department store. Across the way are the neoclassical Revival elements of architect Francis Mawson Rattenbury's former court house, now housing the Vancouver Art Gallery *(see page 25)*. The gallery's rear staircase nicknamed 'Biker's Beach', borders fashionable Robson Street, and is a favourite hang-out for buff-looking bike couriers.

A Leisurely Breakfast

By now it will be time for breakfast. Finding a good place among the underground-mall muffin shops and entrée-priced hotel menus takes some luck and a degree of persistence. Nearby Robson Street known locally as 'Robsonstrasse' has a variety of eateries as well as high-end shops. On the west side of Hornby Street are a number of options that are comfy, sunlit (hopefully) and good: the best is the **Bacchus Ristorante** *(see page 69)*. Or head north (towards the water) to the Fairmont Hotel and Vancouver's best business breakfast location, **Griffins** *(see page 70)*, particularly noted for its Sunday brunch. Inside Cathedral Place you can breeze past the navigating device and glass mural for an unusual breakfast combination. **Carboni Coffee House** has freshly roasted coffee, and you can stop at **Brussels Chocolates**, for an unconventional but sweet breakfast. Dawdle over breakfast with your newspaper – the *Globe and Mail* or the *National Post*, Canada's equivalent to the British *Times*.

Return to the street for a brief lesson in civic and corporate sculpture. At **Cathedral Place** (925 West Georgia Street) look up to see the terracotta gargoyles and art deco sculpted nurses, both recasts from the controversial destruction of the earlier Georgia Medical Dental Building. Across Hornby Street at the **Hong Kong Bank of Canada**, in the enclosed atrium, is **The Pendulum**, a functioning sculpture by Alan Storey that is guaranteed to

Top: the art deco laden Marine Building

mystify. Across Georgia Street is the **Centennial Fountain**, a provincial gift to commemorate the union of Vancouver's *(sic)* Island with the mainland. In full flow, the goddess Diana and a number of seafaring Celts ignore the gushing blasts of 1.3 million litres (343,400 gallons) per hour.

Art and Craft Collections

Back on Hornby Street is the magnificent **Vancouver Art Gallery** (tel: 604 662 4719; daily 10am–5.30pm, Thur until 9pm; admission charge), which has wheelchair access at the front or at Robson Street Plaza, or you can enter on Georgia and Howe streets at the back of the building. Start at the top floor beyond the dome and you can easily spend up to two hours enjoying both the permanent and travelling shows. Take particular note of the **Emily Carr Collection** – more than 40 works by British Columbia's best-known painter. She is said to capture the haunting mysticism of the region's First Nations, particularly the Haida. Among the gallery's unusual features is, they say, a resident ghost – the spirit of Charles Hopkinson, an immigration officer who was murdered in 1914 when the building served as the courthouse.

Walk north on Hornby Street to the postmodern inspired Cathedral Place and find your way through the serene grassed cloister to the **Canadian Craft Museum** (tel: 604 687 8266; Mon–Sat 10am–5pm, Thur until 9pm, Sun noon–5pm; Sept–May: closed Tues). This state-of-the-art space holds an ongoing collection of imaginative Canadian crafts, plus international handmade pieces and rare craft items. Its main gallery features stained glass art by Lutz Haufschild, while the museum shop sells high-quality Canadian ceramics, glassware, jewellery and textiles.

You can lunch early at the **Garden Deli**, a favourite enclave of the office crowd, or continue down Hornby Street. Crossing West Hastings Street take a good look at the 1930s art deco **Marine Building** (355 Burrard Street), long the symbol of Vancouver's emergence as a prosperous port city. Through its arched, ornate door-way is an interior lobby encrusted with terracotta ornamentation, a monument to marine flora and fauna.

On The Waterfront

Hornby Street meets the waterfront at the futuristic white 'sails' of **Canada Place**, intended to resemble a ship. This multi-purpose hotel, office and convention facility now serves the Port of Vancouver's thriving cruise-ship trade, embarking more than half a million passengers on 20 Alaska-bound ocean liners every week between late May and mid-September. Walk along the west promenade for a closer look at these vessels, which might include Holland America Line's MS *Westerdam* – it weighs almost 54,000 tonnes, measures 243m (798ft) in length and carries

Right: an artist at work

1,494 passengers. Many of the newer cruise ships carry up to 3,000 passengers. The *Westerdam* and her five sister ships make the rounds regularly, one of them arriving on average four times a week, docking in the early morning and departing late afternoon.

Once you've reached the Canada Place pier find the plaques listing the Port of Vancouver's history. This is the place to be mesmerised by sweeping views of the harbour, stunning vistas of the port, vast panoramas of mountains and sea, all abuzz with boats, helicopters and float planes.

Reclaimed Heritage

Turn and walk the east side of the pier to Cordova Street and cross to enter the reclaimed heritage **Sinclair Centre** (757 West Hastings Street), which has imaginatively preserved four remarkable buildings joined by a covered atrium. There are some shops here and a few fast lunch restaurants. Pass through, heading east, and regain Cordova Street by entering Gastown's **Waterfront Station**, between Granville and Main streets, site of the 1887 completion of the trans-Canada national railway. It now serves as a terminal that links the public transit SkyTrain, the SeaBus and the West Coast Express train.

History colours your day as you stroll into the site of Vancouver's first European settlement, known as **Gastown**. In 1867 'Portuguese Joe' ran the general store, while with but one barrel of whisky for collateral, loquacious 'Gassy' Jack Deighton built a tavern. Today Gastown is a historic tree-lined commercial district that echoes the free-wheeling days of its pioneers.

A logical starting point is **The Landing** at Water and Cordova streets, once home to a wholesale grocery firm specialising in catering supplies for northbound gold prospectors and now housing an interesting mix of retailers. Take the north side of Water Street and browse. If you're interested in Pacific Northwest and Canadian Inuit art, the **Inuit Gallery** (No 345) and **Hills Native Art** (No 165) are two comprehensive galleries. **The Storyeum** (tel: 604 687 8142), at number 165A, engulfs you in a live presentation of British Columbia's history, complete with memorable characters and legends. Descend one of the world's largest passenger lifts and take the 72-minute guided tour. **La Luna Café** (No 131), has striking yellow-and-black decor, daily papers, coffee and light snacks, making it a pleasant escape from the busy street.

Almost everyone stops to watch the famous **Steam Clock**. The world's first steam-powered timepiece, it has five brass steam whistles that have been hissing tunes at visitors every 15-minutes for more than 100 years.

Top: the renovated Sinclair Building

Cross to the other side of the road and take a look at the iron- and steel-framed **Edward Hotel Building** at 300 Water Street. It was constructed in 1906 and designed to be fire-proof following the 'great fire' that devastated the area *(see page 13)*.

A Labyrinth of Alleyways

At **Maple Tree Square** the whimsical statue of **'Gassy Jack'** standing on a barrel is the main attraction, while Carrall Street leads into increasingly residential Gastown, where housing developments are revitalising the neighbourhood. Turn back to **Gaoler's Mews** at 217 Carrall Street, off Maple Tree Square and Blood Alley Square, both dating from the 1850s. Bloody brawls within the former resulted in incarceration in a small unlocked cabin in the latter. Gastown's first constable, Jonathan Miller, shackled prisoners at the ankle who were then guarded by John Clough, a one-armed drunkard. Today the mews is a pleasant brick-floored alley with ivy-covered walls and a musical carousel clock.

Back on Water Street, return on the city side and explore the restaurants, shops and work spaces. Antiques shops and trendy vintage clothing stores sell wares from bygone eras, and First Nations art and craft galleries and souvenir shops are plentiful. At the intersection of Water and Cordova streets you're on your own. Take a cab back to your hotel or walk the short eight blocks southwest to Robson Square. Along the way you'll find exquisite fountain pens at the **Vancouver Pen Shop Ltd** (512 West Hastings Street).

Downtown Flavour

Aim to finish the day with a quiet drink at the **900 West** lounge and wine bar, at the Fairmont Hotel Vancouver. When it comes to recommendations for dinner, my choice of restaurant in this area would be the sophisticated **Le Crocodile** *(see page 76)*, a warm, rich location that's internationally-renowned and has an Alsace-inspired menu. Other options include **Chartwell** at the Four Seasons Hotel. This restaurant alternates between traditional and contemporary and has great local reviews. **Joe Fortes Seafood and Chop House** *(see page 74)*, with an oyster bar and excellent seafood platters, is very atmospheric – sometimes has a New Orleans jazz band – and always attracts a noisy crowd, especially on Friday and Saturday nights. **Phnom Penh** *(see page 76)*, serves Cambodian, Vietnamese and Chinese cuisine to simple perfection. Try the hot and sour soups and garlic-fried squid.

Right: showers in Gastown

2. STANLEY PARK AND THE WEST END *(see map, p28)*

Take a walking tour of Stanley Park's evergreen forests, seaside paths, mountain views, beaches and gardens. Visit the Vancouver Aquarium Marine Science Centre and the Variety Kids Water Park. Have a Teahouse lunch, then cross the street to a different kind of forest – the high-rise delights of the West End. End the day strolling Denman and Robson streets and eating well.

Our starting point is Robson Square. This is a walking day with taxi or bus assistance if required. For those who like to walk or rent bicycles, dress accordingly. Pack a fresh shirt for the casual but smart Teahouse Restaurant, (brunch or lunch until 2.15pm). For dinner, try Delilah's (no reservations) or Raincity Grill.

Imagine a frontier of nothing but trees: a solid wall of evergreens up to 90m (300ft) high confronting the Vancouver pioneers. They burned them, girdled them and sold them for a dollar apiece – just to see the sky. By 1889 what little remained of the forest within the growing city limits was a military reserve, a peninsula at the mouth of Burrard Inlet – 440 hectares (1,000 acres) of cool, green firs, meadow and beach that, by luck and foresight, became **Stanley Park**. Larger than New York's Central Park, dedicated by

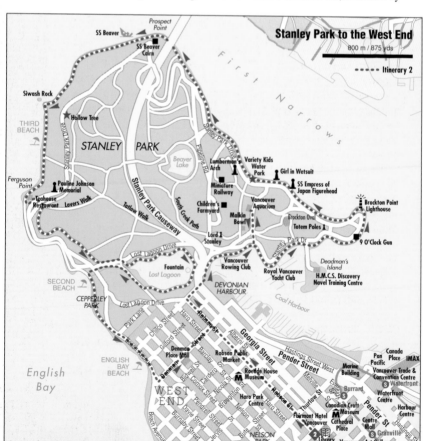

Lord Stanley, Governor General of Canada, only three years after the 1886 incorporation of the city, it is one of the finest parks in the world. To get a full appreciation of this urban wilderness we are going to walk, if not all the way around the park's 8-km (5-mile) perimeter, then at least to some of its most interesting shoreline and forest trails.

Walking down the length of **Robson Street** from **Robson Square**, the park's tall firs and cedars eventually become visible through the steel and concrete canyons of the West End. Take the west side of Robson Street and window shop through a trendy, touristy set of store fronts and casual cafés. A string of high-fashion or chic boutiques, lofts, little restaurants, jewelry and souvenir stores form an eclectic array. Then, dodging not one but two Starbucks coffee houses at Robson and Thurlow streets, choose one of the many java houses to satisfy a caffeine craving – perhaps a cappuccino grandé with wonderful opportunities for people-watching. For breakfast without an attitude try the **Bread Garden Bakery and Café** (812 Bute Street), a half block south of Robson Street. It has fast, take-a-number, service starting at 6am.

Fortified, return to Robson and walk down the hill. Though quiet in the morning, this is one of the most popular streets to stroll in the city: the sidewalks are crowded with all ages, restaurants are five to ten a block, and European- and American-style hotels flank and encroach on the street's shop-and-awning ambiance. As you approach Denman Street you can rent bikes or roller blades from a number of rental shops. Everything is provided at **Bayshore Bicycles and Rollerblade Rentals** (tel: 604 688 2453).

Park Promenade

Walking, riding or rolling, continue on Robson Street to Chilco Street. Take a right and use the tunnel beneath busy Highway 99 to the seawall. Turn left (walkers on the right) to begin your day's exploration of Stanley Park. To your left is the **Lost Lagoon Nature House** (tel: 604 257 8544 for hours) where you can find information on the park's ecology.

Right: *Girl in the Wetsuit*
Top: rollerblading by Stanley Park

On the waterside is the 1911 Tudor-style **Vancouver Rowing Club** and the yachts of the **Royal Vancouver Yacht Club**. Through the masts and rigging the city comes into view. You can take some of your best photographs of the city right here, and most people do. Just beyond the rowing club there's a car park with an information booth. Get a free map of the park – very important because it's easy to get lost in the forest.

If you choose to visit the **Children's Farmyard and Miniature Railway**, continue through the car park and turn left. The railway operates a replica of the first transcontinental passenger train that pulled into Vancouver in the 1880s, and it transports you on a scenic 12-minute ride through an area of cedar and Douglas fir forest.

The **Stanley Park Shuttle**, a free, unguided bus service (late June–mid Sept 10am–6.30pm), departs from the railway every 12–15 minutes and circles 14 of the park's most popular attractions, including Siwash Rock (*see page 31*) and Prospect Point for views over Burrard Inlet, Lions Gate Bridge and the North Shore. You can hop on and off at will along the way.

Nature and History Preserved

To the right of the railway is the wonderful **Vancouver Aquarium Marine Science Centre** (tel: 604 659 3474; Sept–late June: 10am–5.30pm; late June–early Sept: 9.30am–7pm), one of the best of its kind in the world. Here you can do a walk-through of British Columbia's marine environments, plus tropical and Amazonian galleries with piranha, caimans and real rain storms. But the most captivating feature of the aquarium are the snow-white beluga whales, in open-air pools; you can view from the surface or below, through tank-long windows. The aquarium no longer trains these exceptionally intelligent and sociable mammals to entertain, but an Animal Encounters programme allows visitors one-on-one interaction with trainers and animals in replicated natural habitats.

From the aquarium go back to the seawall and turn left to find a thicket of **totem poles** representing the traditions of British Columbia's coastal First Nations people. These valuable poles were saved from destruction in the

period between 1939 and 1950, when totems were not esteemed. Today the artefacts are carefully preserved. Interpretive display panels describe the stories of each individual pole, and a colourful book *Totem Poles*, by Pat Kramer, is available at the shop on site.

Continue around the seawall to **Brockton Point** for a look at the city, the harbour and North Vancouver. The bright yellow pile among the freighters is sulphur; the nearby brown pile is potash. Both are key components in agricultural fertilizers. At the 3km (1½ mile) painted marker – along the base of the seawall curb – is Vancouver's whimsical take on Copenhagen's sculpture, *Little Mermaid* (though this statue is clearly a two-legged woman). The bronze, called *Girl in the Wetsuit (see page 29)*, was created by the artist Elek Imredy and unveiled in 1972. If you have children with you, in another 300m (985ft) they can let off steam in the **Variety Kids Water Park**.

Continue along the park's seawall to the **Lions Gate Bridge**. When the bridge was constructed in 1935, local people feared that it would ruin the serenity of the park but, fortunately, their fears were unfounded. Note the tide. It was tidal action that prevented the siting of one of the earliest sawmills here and helped preserve the land for a park. Stop just past the bridge and study the rock face for a rare, close-up birdwatching experience: cormorants, great ancient fishers, usually nest in the crevices. Here too was the 1888 wreck of the first steamship to sail the Pacific Coast, the Hudson's Bay Company's paddle-wheel trading vessel SS *Beaver*.

Sea Views

Along the seawall path is a volcanic monolith, **Siwash Rock** (6km/4 miles), which according to a Squamish legend, is a love-thwarted First Nations man turned to stone. Just past Third Beach and the next jut of land, **Ferguson Point**, take the steps that hook back up to the lawn and cross it for lunch at the **Teahouse Restaurant** *(see page 69)*. The park setting, view and ambiance (complete with natural light, old wood and white linen) heighten your appetite for a great contemporary menu in a heritage building dating from the days when the park was a military reserve. Choose one of the atriums rather than eating outside if you want to enjoy the view.

From the terrace of the Teahouse call a cab or take a cool forest walk, skirting around the restaurant to your left to enter the woods. Take the trail that parallels the road for 100m (300ft), intersecting Lees trail. Go left following the Bridge Road signs to a 'T', then go right, emerging at Lost Lagoon. Note

Left: a beluga whale at the Vancouver Aquarium
Top: totem poles represent the First Nations

the **Jubilee Fountain**, which was installed in 1936 – it was a left-over from Chicago's World Fair. Circle the fountain and you arrive at a bus loop, where you can catch a ride or walk back up Robson Street to the Square.

Continuing on the seawall path **English Bay** opens up, with Vancouver Island hazy in the distance. At this point you can almost forget you're in a city – until a couple of lycra-clad joggers pass by. English Bay was home to the city's first official lifeguard, Seraphim 'Joe' Fortes, a seaman who was credited with saving many lives from the time of his arrival in the province during the 1880s, until his death in 1922. Today the beach fronts a burgeoning residential area known as the West End.

Eating Out around English Bay

If you're enjoying the sea walk, return to the seawall and continue past the West End high rises. The ivy-clad building on Gilford Street is the cherished, reasonably priced and usually fully booked **Sylvia Hotel** *(see page 88)*. Go one block further and turn onto Denman, a street in flux. On the left is the chic **Raincity Grill** *(see page 70)*, which serves contemporary West Coast cuisine made with the freshest local ingredients, and more than 100 wines by the glass. Across the street are places to sit and sip a latté and watch people pass by. Up the street on the right is the **Clearwater Café**, which specialises in vegetarian food. A block north is a place that really puts the cap on the day – **Delilahs Restaurant and Bar**. Walk right in and put your name on the list, then kill some time by exploring the neighbourhood or sampling the famous martinis to stimulate your appetite. Delilahs doesn't take reservations so the clientele is spontaneous, and dress is casual to elegant. Look up to see the cherubs that dance on the hand-painted ceiling.

On your return up Robson Street, watch strolling couples, tourists and cars crawling at a see-and-be-seen pace. Stop in at a late-night coffeehouse and do some shopping in one of the best night-time street scenes of the city.

Top: stroll around the seawall for spectacular views

3. THE WEST SIDE *(see map, p34)*

The West Side: Granville Island to Point Grey, is a day in the neighbourhoods highlighted by some of the best attractions in the region – the UBC Museum of Anthropology and the Granville Island Market – capped by a dizzying choice of Vancouver's freshest cuisines.

From downtown Robson Square plan on walking or taking a bus to Granville Island Market. Make reservations at CinCin Italian Wood Grill. Plan for a cab back to town.

The feel of quiet, cool, tree-lined streets, the lovingly lived-in Craftsmen bungalows, and the memories made in the bistros are what visitors to the West Side experience. It is Vancouver's experiment in living, its best views, best beaches and widest range of good, friendly, neighbourhoods all strung along Broadway Street and Fourth Avenue.

Granville Island is a taste of Vancouver's rapid evolution from a frontier town to a city on a world scale. Once the site of numerous sawmills and heavy industry, this 15-hectare (38-acre) island is a shrewd, successful and fun collection of farmers' markets, restaurants, small museums, artists' studios and water-related businesses. Granville is situated between the Burrard and Granville street bridges on the south shore of **False Creek**, a saltwater inlet that separates the West End and downtown from the Fairview and Kitsilano neighbourhoods of the West Side.

The 1½-km (1-mile) walk from the hotel district is my personal choice. (If you choose the bus take the number 50 False Creek South on Granville Street and get off at Granville Island.) From any of the hotels west of Granville, go south through the well-manicured, high-rise neighbourhood to Pacific Street, which leads left into Beach Avenue. Beneath the Burrard Street Bridge are small non-polluting passenger mini-ferries (daily; summer: every 5 minutes 7am–11pm; winter: 7am–8pm) that will take you across False Creek: Aquabus (tel: 604 689 5858) and False Creek Ferries (tel: 604 684 7781). Your destination is Granville Island.

The Western Shore

Along Granville Island's western shore **farmers' markets** are similar to London's old Covent Garden and Kuala Lumpur's central markets, with a shed-roofed casbah of vegetable stalls and fruit stalls, take-away booths, fish markets and even a soup stock store. (Local cherries are sometimes heaped on tables, with customers picking through them and tasting them.) From the market turn south and pick up a map at the **Information Centre** (1398 Cartwright Street; tel: 604 666 5784) across the street. There are three small adjoining museums for aficionados nearby: Sports Fishing, Model Ships and Model Trains. Reverse your course past the street

Right: Granville Island marina

entertainment plaza (always good, normally bizarre musicians, jugglers and dancers) and work around the island in a counter-clockwise direction. There are maritime businesses on your right including a boat yard on Duranleau Street, **Ecomarine Ocean Kayak Centre** (tel: 604 689 7575), offering sea kayak retail and rental (*see Itinerary 9: Kayaking in False Creek and English Bay, page 46*).

Street of Culture

On the east side of Duranleau Street the core buildings house the studios of well-known artisans such as: the late Bill Reid, famous for his native carving, abstract painter Gorgon Payne, and Matt Kallio, known for his beautiful cedar chests. They all share neighbouring storefronts around 1659 Duranleau Street. Continue down Duranleau as it bends beneath the bridge. If you're with children, the **Kids' Market** has what's innovative in toys, and just past Old Bridge Street is **Sutcliffe Park**, a perky water park and playground, where your child will be soaked in minutes. Duranleau Street becomes Cartwright Street where the **Gallery of BC Ceramics** signals a knot of craft, glass and fabric galleries inside the circle and the **Emily Carr College of Art and Design** (1399 Johnston Street), on the waterside. You're

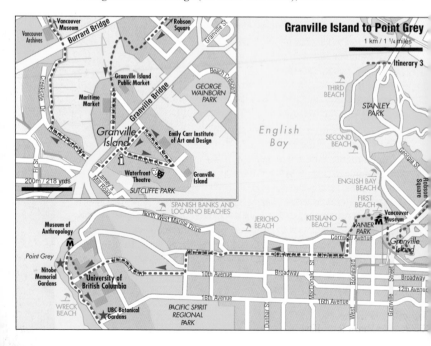

welcome to enter to get a taste of the art students' world and review their work, or visit the **Charles H Scott Gallery** for international exhibitions.

If you fancy a bite to eat try **Bridges Restaurant** *(see page 68)*, which is at full circle just past the ferry dock. Or you can simply walk around the market stalls and pick-up some fresh seafood and bakery goods. But if it's still early and if you're not too hungry, wait for lunch until you reach the eateries along West Fourth Avenue in the hip Kitsilano district.

Vanier Park Museums

Walk along Anderson Street to leave the island. At the end of the causeway (beneath the Granville Street Bridge, note the 'Island Park Walk' sign on the south side of a pylon) walk right (west) along the seawall through the Fairview neighbourhood, with False Creek's commercial fishing boats and yachts on the right. Keep to the path's water side to avoid the roller bladers and bicyclists. In 10 minutes you'll pass beneath the Burrard Street Bridge and spot the **Vanier Park Museum Complex** across a broad lawn. There are three museums from which to pick. Check both the travelling and permanent exhibits in the complex and decide which interests you, or continue your walk westward along the shore. Either way, plan to be back on the seawall by 1–1.30pm.

The **Vancouver Museum** (tel: 604 736 4431; daily 10am–5pm, Thur until 9pm; admission charge) and **H R MacMillan Space Centre** (tel: 604 738 7827; daily 10am–5pm in summer, closed Mon in winter) share the same conical-roofed building (entrance away from the water) at 1100 Chestnut Street. It is designed to resemble a Coast Salish style woven cedar rainhat. The inoffensive (some say bland) Vancouver Museum provides a general look at the history of the city, including **The 50s Gallery** and a number of changing exhibits. The H R MacMillan Space Centre has hands-on exhibits about space exploration, planetarium explorations of the Vancouver sky, laser light shows with rock music, and a *Virtual Voyages* full motion simulator that

will fly you to Mars and back through space and time. You can stargaze on weekend nights (weather permitting) in the separately housed **Gordon MacMillan Southam Observatory** (tel: 604 738 2855) through a 1,000x magnification Cassegrain telescope.

The **Vancouver Maritime Museum** (tel: 604 257 8300; daily 10am–5pm, closed Mon in winter; admission charge), 1905 Ogden Avenue at the foot of Cypress Street, lies a bit west along the shoreline trail. Regain the seawall path and go left (west) to the distinctive A-frame building sheltering the *St Roch*, one of the first ships to navigate the Northwest Passage (the Arctic Ocean) from west to east and to circumnavigate North America. Now that the world's Arctic regions may be melting, this little ship may prove to be

Top left: food for thought
Right: art in Vanier Park, Kitsilano

important evidence in Canada's claims to supremacy in the North. You get to climb aboard the actual RCMP ship and walk through the world of arctic explorers – complete with a very large stuffed walrus.

Kitsilano Beach and English Bay

Return to the seawall west of the museum and walk **Kitsilano Beach**. On any sunny day this is the finest spot in the urban universe – salt water, a wide sky, beach and mountains all at once. The ships anchored offshore in **English Bay** are awaiting berths to load up with one of 30 different grades of wheat, one of Canada's main exports. Across the water is the entrance to Burrard Inlet, West Vancouver, Howe Sound and off to the west, the Sunshine Coast. When the promenade turns toward the neighbourhood, before the 100-m (328-ft) public saltwater pool, cross busy Cornwall Street. If you are fond of Japanese cuisine, try **Kibune Sushi** *(see page 72)* for lunch, a long established authentic restaurant.

Continue walking up Yew Street to Fourth Avenue where there are a couple more restaurants to choose from and which will also get you to the bus stop. Despite the queues, **Sophie's Cosmic Café** *(see page 75)* in a funky neighbourhood bursting with young, grungy energy, is my first choice for today's lunch. **Romios Greek Taverna** *(see page 73)*, the alternative, is a cosy family-run place.

First Nations Culture at the MOA

Catch the westbound No 4 UBC (University of British Columbia) bus on West Fourth Avenue to the University Loop for the Museum of Anthropology. Walk south along University Boulevard through the **University of British**

Columbia campus. The oldest university in BC, incorporated in the first decade of the 20th century, its buildings are something of an architectural hotchpotch but they are set in beautiful grounds, surrounded by trees. Turn right on West Mall Road then north on Marine Drive to the museum – about 1 kilometre (½ mile).

For a look at the rich life of West Coast Native cultures, the **UBC Museum of Anthropology** (tel: 604 822 5087; July–Aug: daily 10am–5pm, until 9pm on Tues; Sept–June: Tues–Sun 11am–5pm, until 9pm on Tues, admission charge) is in many ways the pride of the city. Designed by the internationally honoured local architect Arthur Erickson, the museum (usually known as MOA) is a severe, open, glass-walled, grey concrete space frame, which

Above: at the Museum of Anthropology

encloses some of the finest monumental achievements (totem poles) of the First Nations people of British Columbia. In the main hall you will find superb examples, including massive house posts and burial boxes, carved cedar masks and contemporary carvings of the Kwakwaka'wakw, Tsimshian, Haida, Coast Salish and other bands.

Last comes a collection that is sadly often overlooked, situated in a wing of the museum to the left of the entrance. Yet another coup for the city, this is the superb **Koerner Ceramics Gallery**, a treasurehouse of late 15th- to early 19th-century European pieces of tin-glazed and lead-glazed stoneware and earthenware.

West Side Gardens

Nearby is the **Nitobe Memorial Garden** (tel: 604 822 6038; mid-Mar–mid-Oct: daily 10am–6pm; winter: Mon–Fri 10am–2.30pm; admission charge), set against a pristine forest and meticulously planned by illustrious Japanese experts. Considered one of the few gardens outside of Japan to have achieved its desired level of perfection, it is a so-called tea and stroll garden reflecting an idealized conception of nature. At the corner of 16th Avenue and SW Marine Drive, visitors can enjoy the 28-hectare (70-acre) **UBC Botanical Gardens** (tel: 604 822 4208; daily 10am–6pm; admission charge).

From the university call a cab and either head back to your hotel to change or go east for a stroll through the neighbourhood restaurant and shopping areas on Fourth Avenue between Balsam and Cypress streets, or on Broadway between Alma and Trafalgar streets. If you're travelling by bus, cross the street at MOA and board an eastbound No 42 Chancellor service (hourly, last bus 6.30pm), or backtrack through campus to the bus loop to catch the more frequent eastbound No 4 Powell for Fourth Avenue, or the No 10 Hastings via Broadway. These buses will take you back to town too, so save your transfers.

My choice for dinner is the **CinCin Italian Wood Grill** *(see page 69)*, an al fresco *delecto* wrapped in sultry Tuscan tones, perfect for a flirtatious, yet sophisticated evening.

Top: out on the town

4. CHINATOWN *(see map, p22)*

If there's one place in Vancouver that transports you to another world, to pungent markets and the voices of many countries, it's Chinatown. Spend the morning in the markets and shops, visit a classical Chinese garden and sample *dim sum* at lunchtime.

Take a taxi to the Millennium Gate at East Pender and Taylor, or walk the Silk Road from the Public Library. Mid-morning is the best time to arrive.

Gumshan was the word that spread throughout the Pearl River region of Southeast China, bringing labourers and merchants to the 'Gold Mountain' of North America. They came first during the California Gold Rush of 1849 and then 10 years later to the Fraser River and the so-called Cariboo gold fields of British Columbia. The Chinese proved willing and resourceful, often the only reliable source of labour in the region. They worked the timber mills in the 1860s, they canned salmon along the Fraser, and from 1881–85 they came en masse to build the British Columbia section of the Canadian Pacific Railway. In Vancouver the Chinese (mainly from Canton) settled just east of the Hastings Mill area, first in shacks but by the turn of the 20th century in a distinctive Chinese-style, brick-built business district they called Saltwater City, in time known simply as Chinatown.

Today **Chinatown**, with more recent immigrants from Hong Kong, is an historical, sensual and active community. Bordered by Hastings, Keefer, Gore (Avenue) and Taylor streets, it's accessible via the **Silk Road**, a walking route from downtown marked by colourful signs, which starts at the **Vancouver Public Library** (350 West Georgia Street) and leads through Keefer Street, the International Village, Millennium Gate, the Chinese Cultural Centre, the Chinatown market, and Dr Sun Yat-Sen Classical Chinese Garden.

A Sense of the Past

East Pender Street has a real sense of the past. Street signs are bilingual and shop window scripts include Cantonese and Mandarin. The architecture is of narrow three-, four- and five-storey buildings with recessed balconies (to watch dragon parades) and Chinese ornamentation. The upper floors of benevolent societies provided early immigrants with a respite from the racism of the 20th century. Many of the old gaming parlours and opium dens are now insurance and accountants' offices, while the upstairs restaurants still serve *dim sum* and markets spill out onto the street. The gaily painted **Millennium Gate** stands at the entrance to the **Chinese Cultural Centre** (50 East Pender Street, tel: 604 658 8850) where seasonal exhibitions extol the prevalent Asian cultures. Nearby is the **Dr Sun Yat-Sen Classical Chinese Garden** (578 Carrall Street at Pender, tel: 604 689 7133; daily 10am–4.30pm; admission charge). This is the first full-sized Suzhou style classical garden constructed outside China. Built with traditional materials

Left: Asian warmth

and tools, it is a re-creation of a scholars' retreat of the 14th- and 15th-century Ming period. In such places ancient philosophers sought enlightenment in harmony with nature. Guided walking tours of Chinatown also originate from this point and they are recommended. Ask the attendant about the summertime **Chinatown Night Market** (Fri–Sun 6.30–11pm), at 100 and 200 block Keefer Street, where stalls are piled high with food and other goodies. Feel free to barter with the stallholders. Continue west, crossing Carrall Street, to the 'thinnest' building in the world, according to Ripley's, Believe It or Not! The **Sam Kee Building** (8 West Pender Street) is only 1.8m (6ft) wide. Take a photo in front of the massive **Han Dynasty Bell** in the **Shanghai Alley** outdoor 'museum', then cross Pender Street to window shop in the curio stores. At the **Fine Art Treasury** (101 East Pender Street) you can order a marble Chinese horoscope stamp: carved with your animal sign and your name in Cantonese.

A World of Markets

East of Main Street the **Fresh Market** stretches from Gore Avenue to Hastings Street. You'll see hundreds of shoppers – mostly Asian, including Chinese, Vietnamese, Cambodian and Korean. The pavements are narrow, grandmothers are bartering and children are effortlessly flowing through the throng, while the noise of humanity mingles with the scent of the true markets of the world. You could well be in Guangzhou (Canton). Wicker baskets, tubs and bins are filled with fresh local *yau choy*, *bau choy* (Chinese greens) and *yui mo qua* (squash). In summer there's foul-smelling sweet durian and hairy *rambutangs* from Thailand and Malaysia. There are mangosteens, longan and lychees, and interestingly named *ping gwoal* (apple) and *fun see* (noodles).

At **Kam Tong Enterprises** the catch is alive and includes eels, delicate blue crabs, local geoducks (pronounced 'gooey-ducks'), which are large clams, gooseneck barnacles and razor clams (beware: they squirt.) The **Dollar Meat Store** (266 East Pender Street) has the famous barbeque- and pressed-ducks, plus home-made Chinese sausages, trays of beef tendon and lung, and chicken feet. Stop for a drink at **Live Like Water** (104–633 Main Street), a tranquil tea house, where you sit on cushions or tiny stools and savour one of the high mountain hand-picked teas.

Continue to 261–69 Keefer Street to the **Kiu Shun Trading Co**. **Ltd**, a Chinese apothecary selling ginseng, deer's horn and medicinal herbs. Amidst signs in Chinese, English and French, registered herbalists demystify Chinese medicine. Stop in at either the **New Town Bakery & Restaurant** (158 East

Top: Dr Sun Yat-Sen Classical Chinese Garden

Pender Street) or the **Boss Bakery and Restaurant** (532–34 Main Street) and try the delicious *guy may bow* (coconut buns), savory steamed pork buns, almond cookies or layered red bean pastries. Steamed buns are salty or sweet, spicy or plain, meaty or vegetarian.

End your Chinatown morning in local style with some *dim sum* at **Park Lock Seafood Restaurant** *(see page 71)* on Main Street, but do it well before 1pm to get the best selection. Choose from the wheeled carts that are pushed around the tables: steamed or fried dumplings, meat-, seafood- or vegetable-filled pastries (your bill reflects the number of portions you choose). To return take a taxi back to your hotel.

5. WEST VANCOUVER *(see map, p18–19)*

Either take a morning walk along the seawall and have lunch at Dundarave Beach, or visit the old-growth coastal forest trails at Lighthouse Park and eat at Horseshoe Bay.

If you wish to follow both options in one day you should rent a car. Otherwise take a 'blue' West Vancouver bus from downtown.

Head for **Ambleside Park**, just west of the Lions Gate Bridge, where a playground beside the seawalk is ideal for kids who want to play in the warm sand or dip in the ocean. Ambleside Beach marks the beginning of the **West Vancouver Centennial Seawalk**, with a separate dog trail behind a wire fence. Follow the seemingly ageless joggers taking in the grand view of the suspension bridge, built in 1938 by the Guinness family to enhance their cosmopolitan West Van property holdings – part 'Miami pink stucco', with shoreside high-rise condos, part-Mediterranean, with villas commanding rocky sea coves. This neighbourhood is right on the

Top: traditional medicinal herbs on sale
Left: fun in the sun

sea, yet sequestered deep in the rainforest, where the average house price has risen to more than US$850,000.

High on the mountainside above, black bears are a seasonal nuisance – especially on refuse collection days. It is not unusual for neighbourhood children to be confronted by a bear on their way to school, so they are taught at an early age how to deal with the animals: remain quiet, back away slowly, and do not run away as prey would. To date there have been no human casualties, but each year up to 65 bears are shot and killed when they wander into North Shore residential areas; conservation officers don't respond to bear sightings unless the animals are reported to be aggressive.

For 2km (1½ miles) enjoy the shipping traffic, a few signed detours into the neighbourhood, then back to the seaside and the delightful family beach at the foot of 24th Street and Marine Drive, called **Dundarave Park**.

Just up a block is a great mural by Jim McKenzie depicting the 1792 British and Spanish meeting off Stanley Park – showing not only a land carpeted with forest but also just where the old Squamish and Musqueam villages were situated. Behind that wall is **Capers Community Market** (2496 Marine Drive, tel: 604 925 3316), where the best and healthiest organically grown food is presented in a small and comfortable space. The market also has an espresso machine and a good deli counter. Through the back of the store and up the stairs is a fine, casual and healthy lunch spot, **Capers Café**, with a deck that catches the sun. Stop here for breakfast or lunch, depending on your watch.

Lighthouse Park

For a second walking adventure, this time deep within a coastal old-growth forest, visit **Lighthouse Park**. Cross Marine Drive and catch the westbound No 250 Horseshoe Bay bus and enjoy the drive through a neighbourhood of forest homes. The bus stop you need will come up suddenly, so when you board the bus ask the driver to let you know when you arrive. Walk down the suburban Beacon Lane into the park and towards **Point Atkinson**. Pick one of the two main trails to the lighthouse and loop back on the other for a beautiful 5-km (3-mile) forest walk that incorporates the transition from the dry Coastal Douglas Fir Zone to the wetter Coastal Western Hemlock Zone.

Back on Marine Drive catch the bus again, continue west to **Horseshoe Bay**, a snug harbour tucked into the place where Vancouver runs out of room and the Coast Range meets the sea. The **BC Ferry Terminal** that routes ferries to Vancouver Island's Nanaimo and the Sunshine Coast takes up much of the town's remaining space. It is touristy, but it still manages a fine waterfront park with a few totem poles and good fish and chips at **Troll's** *(see page 74)*, overlooking the lovely park and the crowded harbour. Return to Vancouver by the No 257 or the No 250 bus from the ferry terminal.

Right: Lighthouse Park

6. THE MORNING OF THE FUTURE *(see map, p18–19)*

Have breakfast in the architecturally flamboyant Canada Place district, visit TELUSphere, a hands-on science museum, then board the SkyTrain to New Westminster Quay for a fun picnic lunch beside the river.

Set out before breakfast and take a taxi or use public transport to reach Robson Square. Bring a picnic lunch.

Vancouver's penchant for newness, imagination and ingenuity continues unabated. Already accustomed to remarkably adventurous and at times bizarre architecture, high-speed ferries and high-tech lifestyles, Vancouverites take for granted the fact that their city looks like the cover of *Popular Science* magazine. The Expo '86 World's Fair theme of transport brought the city more: a new port of entry for the growing cruise ship trade, a transport hub and a light-rail system to speed you on your morning's adventure.

Start with a walk from Robson Square north on Howe Street towards **Canada Place** and its distinctive rooftop 'sails' for a leisurely breakfast gazing at the harbour from **Herons** (tel: 604 691 1818) in the Fairmont Waterfront Hotel lobby. Don't be surprised if you see a large cruise ship berthed at Canada Place, because Vancouver is the main southern terminus for vessels sailing north to Alaska during the summer. Travel east to the renovated **Waterfront Station** at 601 West Cordova Street, for the **SkyTrain**. Buy a ticket for **New Westminster**, but get off at the **Main Street Station** and keep your ticket for later. Head in the direction of the silver geodesic dome on Quebec Street, nicknamed the 'golf ball' and now the site of **TELUSphere** (tel: 443 7443; summer: daily 10am–6pm; winter: Mon–Fri 10am–5pm, Sat and Sun 10am–6pm; admission charge).

TELUSphere is a kids' world, a multi-level, almost totally interactive mix of science disguised as fun – from fun-house mirrors and computers (always busy), to plasma balls, floating magnets, robotics, mind puzzles and music machines. If you're travelling with kids expect to spend two hours there; adult

Top: skyline view of the Holiday Inn and the Science Museum.

groups probably one hour. Back on the eastbound SkyTrain enjoy the suburbs with a view of the Fraser River en route to **New Westminster Quay**.

The first major project to bring sophisticated places to the river's edge, the
quay is patterned after Granville Island. The upper levels of the market are
given over to shopping and deck restaurants, while the main floor is a true
farmer's market with a mix of take-aways as well. Picnic along the river wall
where, from time to time, the 100-passenger MV *Native* (tel: 604 525 4465)
cruises along the Fraser River. Take the SkyTrain back to Waterfront Station.

7. GARDENS OF PRIDE *(see map, p18–19)*

**Vancouverites are serious about their gardens, and these four West
Side gardens really stand out, ranging from formal to natural, from
tiny to more than 40 hectares (99 acres). They are as beautiful as they
are indicative of the people and their pride of the city.**

*Buses (transit Information line: tel: 604 521 0400) will get you to each
garden, but this itinerary is best done by car (bring coins for parking meters).
From downtown drive across either bridge south, then go west on Fourth
Avenue, which becomes Chancellor Boulevard, then SW Marine Drive. Make
dinner reservations at Seasons in the Park restaurant.*

The **Nitobe Memorial Garden** (1903 West Mall, UBC Campus, tel: 604
822 6038; mid-Mar–mid-Oct: daily 10am–5pm, to 6pm mid-May–early
Sept; winter: Mon–Fri 10am–3pm; admission charge), a formal Japanese
garden, is a quiet place to begin. It is just 100m (330ft) up Marine Drive from
the **UBC Museum of Anthropology** *(see page 36)*. A memorial to Inazo
Nitobe, Japan's noted educator on East–West détente, this serene garden is
a carefully tended forest walk circling a carp-filled lake and pond. Shaded
in a grove of tall firs is a large and graceful stone Kashuga-style lantern,
one of many on the paths signifying the origins of the Japanese people.
Some of these lanterns are female, others are male – for Adam and Eve – with

unexpected similarities to the myths at the
neighbouring Museum of Anthropology. Ask
the gatekeeper for more information.

Food for Thought

Squashes, marigolds, chocolate cosmos, Aunt
Molly's ground cherries in raised beds, this
is a vegetable garden to die for. Called simply 'Food Garden', it is just one of 10 unique
gardens in the sprawling 47-hectare (116-acre)
UBC Botanical Gardens *(see page 37)*.
There's also a medicinal ('physick') garden of
therapeutic plants, with labels providing not
only their Latin and common names but also
the reputed uses for each plant.

A native plant garden represents all of
British Columbia – from the prickly pear

Right: the Nitobe Memorial Garden

cactus of the Gulf Islands to the alpine flowers of the Stikine Mountains, and there's even a winter garden that inspires Vancouver's gallant year-round gardeners with new hardy varieties of roses, irises and pansies. The gardens are all connected by a series of paths and trails that draw you to the variety and beauty of the flora; more than 400 species of rhododendron bloom during May and June in the Asian garden alone.

Drive east on SW Marine Drive to the 'Y', taking West 41st Avenue to Oak Street. Turn left and left again on West 37th to park. Here, the **VanDusen Botanical Garden** (tel: 604 878 9274; daily from 10am, closing times vary) is located in the Shaughnessy neighbourhood. The garden, which is undergoing a multi-million dollar facelift, has 22 hectares (54 acres) of flora from around the world. In bloom year-round, it features an Elizabethan Maze, Laburnum Walk, a Sino-Himalayan Garden, Canadian Heritage Area, Kitchen Gardens and five small lakes. In this rambling country garden of sculpted beds, you will find the largest late-spring collection of rhododendron in Canada, a well-tended rose garden in summer, a fragrance garden and even a corner that is going to seed – turning rural in a controlled manner – best in mid- to late-summer. **Shaughnessy Restaurant** *(see page 71)*, located at the garden's main entrance, has a heated outdoor deck for year-round dining.

The Royal Garden

Queen Elizabeth Park, named for the late Queen Mother in honour of her 1939 visit to the city, is less than 1.6km (1 mile) east. Go east on West 37th Avenue to Cambie Street, turn left then right on West 33rd Avenue. Once an old rock quarry and – at 150m (492ft) – still the highest point within city limits, the park is the city's formal garden and has one of its best views. All 50 hectares (120 acres), including an arboretum, are beautifully manicured. Trails weave through the old quarries past 15-m (50-ft) waterfalls and grottoes filled with blooms. Roses, azaleas and rhododendron often provide the backdrop for the popular Asian wedding photo sessions. At the top of the hill in the park is the **Bloedel Floral Conservatory** (tel: 604 257 8570; admission charge), a humid equatorial jungle of exotic plants, screeching macaws and free-flying tropical birds under a sky-lit geodesic-dome.

When it's near sunset, stop at the elegant **Seasons in the Park** restaurant (tel: 604 874 8008) on Cambie Street at West 33rd Avenue, either for a drink or for the dinner which you reserved earlier, and to admire the view of Vancouver. To return to downtown take Cambie Street north into town.

Top: Queen Elizabeth Park is popular for wedding photo sessions
Right: Kitsilano Beach

8. VANCOUVER'S BEACHES *(see map, p18–19)*

Whether you stroll or sunbathe, swim or people-watch, you'll find Vancouver's in-city beaches exceptional. Enjoy both sides of English Bay, the grand vistas of Spanish Banks and the eccentricity of the swimsuit-optional Wreck Beach.

For Kitsilano, take the Aquabus from Sunset Beach to the Maritime Museum landing. To reach Wreck Beach by bus from town take the No 4 or 10 to the University Loop and walk west through the campus; from the Locarno beach hostel take the No 42 bus. Bring swimwear, beach mats, sunscreen and walking shoes. Parking is difficult at Wreck Beach.

Vancouver – the beach? Despite a latitude about the same as London's, this is a city of delightful sandy beaches – ten, in fact – stretching from Stanley Park out and around Point Grey. In the summer you can swim, but for most people a few frantic strokes is enough, as the water temperature rarely exceeds 18°C (65°F). The closest beach within walking distance of the hotel district is **Sunset** or **First Beach** on Pacific Avenue, fronting English Bay between Gilford and Nicola. **Second Beach** is just inside Stanley Park and is family oriented with a great outdoor wading pool. **Third Beach** is one of the prettiest and most secluded along the south shore of the Stanley Park seawall. These beaches are quick to get to, but the best beaches are further along, across False Creek on the West Side.

Pride of the Neighbourhood

From the Maritime Museum landing, walk west along a shoreside promenade to **Kitsilano Beach**. This is a broad, sandy beach angled into the afternoon sun, the pride of the neighbourhood, with a generous park leading off to the residences and a string of good take-aways on Cornwall Street between Laburnum and Cypress streets, including **Planet Veg** *(see page 77)*. On the beach there are concessions and changing rooms (as there are at most of the city beaches) and the quite remarkable 137-m (450-ft) long outdoor saltwater **Kitsilano Pool** (2305 Cornwall Avenue, tel: 604 731 0011; summer only; admission charge), one of 17 public pools in the city.

city itineraries

Sands and Trails

Jericho, **Locarno** and **Spanish Banks** comprise one great strand with two long, sandy northwest-facing beaches. Grassy fields beyond the beach are filled with volleyball parties at weekends. Walk west from Kitsilano Beach along Point Grey Road to Jericho. With 45 hectares (111 acres) of upland lawn and mature maples meeting English Bay, Locarno is a favourite picnic beach, while Jericho Beach is the site of the 285-bed Vancouver International Youth Hostel (tel: 604 224 3208). From Spanish Banks, named for the 1792

meeting between the Spanish explorers Galiano and Valdés and British Captain George Vancouver, the view back to the city, mountains and sky takes your breath away. The trail that separates the beach from the lawns is considered to be one of the best jogs in North America.

Lastly, go to Vancouver's most loved, eccentric and vilified **Wreck Beach** for a return to the 1960s and an education in tourism. Come prepared to take some clothes off and enjoy the community spirit. This is a clothing-optional naturists' beach, grudgingly acknowledged by the city, though it has been a place for well-tanned free spirits since the 1920s. Up to 12,000 people sun themselves here on a hot weekend. Don't take pictures unless you ask permission first.

Wreck Beach is not on the map. Located below NW Marine Drive, west of the Museum of Anthropology, look for the collection of mountain bikes. Angled right into the midday summer sun at the end of Point Grey, the beach is 6.5sq. km (2½sq. miles) of fun. You can take a rough 237-stair trail down through a tangled bluff forest, pick a suitable log to lean against and pull out a William Burroughs novel. Vendors, ethical if not quite legal, sell Caesar salads and whole pink grapefruits injected with 151-proof Jamaican rum.

9. KAYAKING IN ENGLISH BAY *(see map, p18–19)*

In the heart of the city, on Granville Island, sea kayaking is a fun way to explore the skyline along the shores of False Creek and English Bay.

Take a short walk or bus ride from Robson Square to Granville Island (see page 33) bring a windbreaker, sunglasses and sun screen. Consider this activity only if you are a strong swimmer and have boating experience.

Pick a nice afternoon and take a reliable friend along to the **Ecomarine Ocean Kayak Centre** (tel: 604 689 7575), on Granville Island just west of the main market off Duranleau Street, where you'll be instructed, outfitted and launched. Once familiar with the kayak and equipment, you get a quick lesson on paddling, getting in and out, basic rescue and where to go – all in about 10 minutes. Choose a two-hour paddling session, or a 2½-hour guided paddle, which departs three times each day. The price includes safety equipment.

On the water, paddle slowly out through the piers of fishing boats and yachts, keeping to the right. Off Granville Island you enter **False Creek** – it's

Above: sunset over the sea

a busy channel, so be careful – filled with racing dragon boats, sloops and power boats, and the aquabuses shuttling to and fro. Steer right along Granville's shore beneath the Granville Street Bridge. To your right is **Sea Village**, one of the few houseboat communities in the city. Past that the 1970s condos of the Fairview Slopes march up the hill toward the **City Hall** and the Vancouver General Hospital. At the eastern end of False Creek you will see the landmark stainless steel 'golf ball', a remnant of Expo '86, now the TELUSphere 'hands-on museum' *(see Itinerary 6, page 42).*

Turning back along the north shore, you will see the construction that signals the influence and power of Vancouver's Hong Kong community. High-rise housing and offices with urban amenities that include parks and a **Bikeway** (tel: 604 871 6070, Bicycle Hotline), that runs from Stanley Park all the way around False Creek to the Point Grey beaches.

English Bay

Cross under the three bridges and paddle out into English Bay. Check the weather – it's windier out here – and check your rental time, too.

English Bay was where George Vancouver's ships anchored to chart Burrard Inlet and False Creek. Follow the beaches on your right and come ashore for a stretch, if the weather permits. This is First Beach – not quite in Stanley Park and more of a neighbourhood beach for the West End.

Back in your kayak, head across the mouth of the bay to the Kitsilano side and the moored historical ships at the foot of the tall A-framed **Maritime Museum** (1905 Ogden Avenue, tel: 604 257 8300), in Vanier Park. Old tugboats, schooners, the *Black Duck* RCAF rescue vessel, and various classic boats (some you can visit) are all on display. Turn east and paddle beneath the Burrard Street Bridge. It was here on the southern shore that the Squamish Indian village of Snauq (meaning 'inside, at the head') was nestled up against the forest. At **Bridges** (you'll see the sign) turn in and return your kayak. Then head for the deck at **Bridges Pub** (1551 Johnston Street, tel: 604 687 7351) for a Granville Island Pale Ale.

Top: ready for some action on the water

10. THE NORTH SHORE *(see map, p18–19)*

Take the SeaBus ferry to the North Shore for views of the city and the working harbour. Explore Lonsdale Quay, have lunch, then teeter across the Capilano Suspension Bridge and ride the gondola up Grouse Mountain for the best upland views of the city.

Take the SeaBus from Waterfront Station, at the foot of Seymour Street, adjacent to the Pan Pacific Centre, for an hour and 40-minute ride across Burrard Inlet. Make a reservation for Altitudes Bistro on Grouse Mountain, which gets you the Skyride for free. Bring hiking boots.

The ferry landing is also a connection for buses to 'North Van' and 'West Van', the dormitory communities that are steadily encroaching on the forest. But before you hop on a bus to the edge of the woods, check the schedule and then take some time to explore the engaging **Lonsdale Quay Market** (123 Carrie Cates Court, tel: 604 985 2191), a bustling and colourful mix of vegetable stalls, fresh fish sellers and take-away kiosks, with clothing, curio and toy shops, right on the waterfront.

It is a rare city that integrates its working harbour with any kind of public access, but the quay has a broad, open-piered square with the SeaBus terminal on the right and the Deas Towboat company piers on the left. Have lunch (try

take-away from The Stock Pot or Dex Gourmet Burger Bar) and watch the staunch little harbour tugs come and go while mammoth grain ships and container freighters glide past you towards their berths. Nearly 10,000 local and foreign ships arrive here every year, so you can expect to see more than 25 ships a day transiting the harbour.

Beyond the market at the foot of Lonsdale Avenue is a lovely little Greek restaurant: **Anatoli Souvlaki** *(see page 73)*. You could have a late lunch here or book for dinner. Up Lonsdale Avenue and right on First Avenue you can wander through the nearby flea market to browse its oddities and meet its characters. Return now to the SeaBus terminal for the next stop – at the forest primeval.

Treetop Views

The Grouse Mountain bus (No 236) runs through a residential district of North Vancouver that was once perpetually shaded by 100-m (330-ft) tall fir, hemlock and cedar trees. The massive trees fed the many mills that rimmed Burrard Inlet and False Creek, until the suburbs were invented. But where the Capilano River cuts deep en route to Burrard Inlet, many of the less accessible trees escaped the fate of their flatland brethren.

The pulse-quickening **Capilano Suspension Bridge** (3735 Capilano Road, tel: 604 985 7474), was one of the earliest of Vancouver's tourist attractions, and a treetop viewing area in the cedar forest has been added. The bridge is 140m (450ft) of undulating steel cable and planking over a breathtaking

Above: harbour tug
Right: a treetop view from Capilano Suspension Bridge

70-m (230-ft) drop to the Capilano River. It's worth the crossing, not only for the vertigo but also to observe the variety of human reactions it causes. The first totem poles you see were carved in the 1930s by two Danish immigrants; the more recent additions are by local First Nations peoples.

Just 200m (655ft) up the highway is **Capilano River Regional Park** (daily from 9am), which is always crowded during high season. It is perhaps the finest forest in the city, with paths trailing along the steeply flowing river. (Listen for the trill of the winter wrens and chickadees, and occasional robins.) If you're walking, take care at the narrow road entry to the park, and in about 200m (220yds) take the signed 'pipeline' trail into the **Capilano Salmon Hatchery** (tel: 604 666 1790). This is also a jump-off point to **Capilano Lake** and the maze of trails looping back to the bridge. Get a trail map. If you're driving, there's ample parking at the hatchery.

A Ride to the Sky

Back on Nancy Green Way (named for Canada's first Olympic gold medalist in skiing) check the sky. If it's clear, continue uphill on the Grouse Mountain bus for 10 minutes to **Grouse Mountain** and its 100-passenger aerial tram, **Skyride** (tel: 604 980 9311; daily 9am–10pm). It whisks you up 1,130m (3,700ft), for an amazing view (and skiing in the winter). Below, Vancouver looks tiny, and beyond the city the panorama takes in Vancouver Island and the Olympic Peninsula Mountains in Washington State, USA. At the summit is the **World Famous Lumberjack Show**, the **Refuge for Endangered Wildlife**, **Birds in Motion** demonstrations and nature trails. Those in good physical condition can hike a trail, called the **Grouse Grind**, or Mother Nature's Stairmaster, begins just to the right of the car park entrance and ascends – seemingly straight up – about 3km (2 miles) through rock-strewn forest, a gruelling 2-hour, sometimes alarming, scramble of 853m (2,800ft).

From the deck of **Altitudes Bistro** *(see page 68)* on a clear day even volcanic Mount Rainier in Washington, USA, 230km (140 miles) south, can be seen. Return to Vancouver on the tram (after 6.30pm the transit runs back to the SeaBus terminal every hour).

Excursions

1. VICTORIA *(see map, p53)*

Victoria is an island city, a romantic, quaint and historic seaport. As your floatplane glides towards the inner harbour, yachts pass beneath, readying for sea, and the grand Parliament buildings vie with the imposing Empress Hotel for your attention. You step ashore to the fragrance of roses mingled with salty sea air, to a festive mood and an air of unhurried ease. This excursion takes you to the Maritime Museum, Victoria's Chinatown, the Royal British Columbia Museum and the stunning Butchart Gardens.

This excursion does not require a car. Plan for a day, overnight or, better still, two nights. Book a mid-morning flight with Pacific Coastal Airlines (tel: 604 273 8666), West Coast Air Service (tel: 604 606 6888; 604 299 9000 ext 6888) or Helijet Airways (tel: 604 273 1414 or 1 800 665 4354), and ask for port (left) side seats. By bus via BC Ferries, take Pacific Coach Lines (tel: 604 662 7575), 3½ hours. The Fairmont Empress Hotel (tel: 1 800 441 1414), is the place to stay. Reserve rooms for one or two nights and a table at the Empress Dining Room, or try the delightful but somewhat remote Sooke Harbour House (tel: 250 642 3421). By car, just take the ferry (tel: 1 888 223 3779).

Victoria is a city that once dominated the frontier of British Columbia. Settled in 1843 by the Hudson's Bay Company, the choice for the site was a political one – to secure England's border with the United States. Little thought was given to its island isolation as everyone then travelled by ship, and the Hudson's Bay Company was never one to encourage settlers to interrupt its valuable fur trade. When gold was discovered in the British Columbia interior in 1858, Victoria flourished. But in the 1890s, at the height of its Victorian era, Vancouver's transcontinental railway and ports lured away its business and its growing populace. The capital city slowed its pace, tending its gardens and its fading glory for a long, quiet century.

Garden City

Victorians are good gardeners, proud of the 1,000 or so flower baskets that festoon their public areas, and have nurtured their heritage well. Today the city is set apart from 'mere mortal cities' (as one tour-bus driver remarked) by its colonial character and its location on the very southern tip of Vancouver Island. The waters that separated Victoria from the head-long growth of Vancouver and Seattle – the Georgia Strait and the Strait of Juan de Fuca – now insulate the city from Vancouver's commercial hustle, making it a wonderful place to live, and an unusually seductive experience for any visitor.

GRAY LINE TOURS

Left: the Parliament Building at dusk
Right: get on the bus

Victoria by Air

The beauty of a Victoria weekend begins with the ease of getting there. The floatplanes take off right next to Canada Place for the 35-minute flight, while Helijet boards just east of the old Canadian Pacific Railway Station. Leaving Vancouver's harbour, note that you're flying in one of Canada's best inventions, a plane evolved from the hardy bush planes that still serve the remote regions of the Northern Territories. The pilot will usually fly right over the Lions Gate Bridge and English Bay and then set a course across the generally calm, protected waters of the Georgia Strait. Weaving through the

Gulf Islands, watch for pods of Orcas while travelling through some of the best maritime scenery in the world. Below you is the gulf and the US San Juan Islands, then the broad expanse of the Strait of Juan de Fuca. You may be able to see in the distance the Olympic Mountains in Washington State, USA. In 30 minutes the plane banks, lands and docks right against Victoria's inner harbour seawall.

The Inner Harbour

You will want to linger around the harbour, for this is not simply a port of arrival, it's both the heart and the pulse of the city. Victoria has one of the loveliest natural harbours in the world, and there's always a bustle of activity on the water, from leisure craft, whale-watching and sightseeing boats to ferries and floatplanes. There is a string of tourist attractions, such as an aquarium and waxworks, around the waterfront, and on fine summer days there's a real buzz from the throngs of visitors and street per-formers. Lending a stately grandeur to the scene are two of the city's finest buildings: the flamboyant domed **Parliament Buildings** (summer: daily 8.30am–4.30pm; winter: Mon–Fri only) and the huge, chateau-style **Fairmont Empress Hotel**, noted (some say overrated) for its afternoon tea. Start the day by having breakfast buffet-style at **Kipling's**, in the Empress Hotel, or walk across Humboldt Street to **Sams Deli** (805 Government Street) for fresh muffins and coffee.

Victoria is even more compact than Vancouver so exploring on foot is easy. It's sunnier here than in Vancouver, too, with nearly a third less rain: 619mm (24 inches) to Vancouver's 1,588mm (62 inches) annually. **Gray Line Tours** (tel: 250 388 5248; every half-hour), use bright red, English-built, double-decker buses, which leave from the front of the Empress on a 1½-hour narrated

Above: the harbour with the Fairmont Empress Hotel in the background
Right: the Tea Lobby

tour of the city and its neighbourhoods. Unfortunately there is not a hop on-and-off option and so buses tend to be rather cramped; avoid it on a hot day.

A National Treasure

Just a few steps from the harbour, is the **Royal British Columbia Museum** (675 Belleville Street, tel: 250 387 3014; daily 10am–5.30pm; admission charge), considered to be one of the best museums in North America. Using dioramas and recreations, with a superb collection of artefacts, the museum covers the natural history of BC as well as its historic role and social development. You'll see George Vancouver's great ship's cabin as it was in 1792, a Kwa-gulth winter long-house, an uncannily lifelike forest to walk through, as well as a turn-of-the-20th century town, innovative films and a full-sized mammoth. Best of all are its groundbreaking First Nations displays, which provide a telling comparison between the people's lives before and after colonisation. It's definitely worth taking the audio tour.

Thunderbird Park, beside the museum, has an array of totems. You can also visit the **National Geographic IMAX** cinema and several **Heritage Houses** (tel: 250 387 4697; daily in summer.) in the care of the museum, including the restored girlhood home of West Coast painter and author Emily Carr.

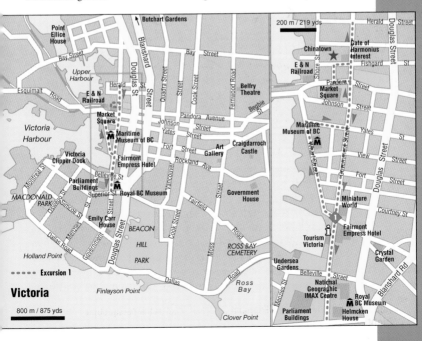

Exploring Downtown

Back on the harbour, cross **Government Street** at Wharf Street and look left for a great view of the 1895 Parliament Buildings, which are illuminated at night. Stop at the art deco **Tourism Victoria** building (812 Wharf Street, tel: 250 953 2033) for a map and information, then follow the shoreline. Several fishing, whale-watching and sea-kayaking excursions depart from the dock on the left side of the street. On the right, at 1107 Wharf Street, is a kids' favourite, the **Victoria Bug Zoo** (tel: 250 384 2847), where exotic insects can be handled.

At Bastion Square the **Maritime Museum of British Columbia** (tel: 250 385 4222; daily 9.30am–4.30pm; admission charge), with its 5,000 nautical artefacts, reflects the importance of seafaring in the history of the province. Its imaginative displays cover early seafaring explorers, the waves of immigrants who arrived by sea in search of a better life, and the development of maritime trade routes. Not surprisingly, there's a section devoted to the Hudson's Bay Company, which played a large part in opening up Canada's remote areas. There are also displays on whaling and fishing, pirates, shipwrecks, the Canadian Navy and BC Ferries.

From here, go north (left) on Government Street, to explore Victoria's **Chinatown**, with its beautiful **Gates of Harmonious Interest** – they say the lions that adorn the gates will come alive the day a totally honest person walks between them. Once a district of gambling houses and opium factories, this is now a fascinating area, with shops selling Asian goods along Fisgard Street and tiny Fan Tan Alley, the narrowest street in Canada. One block further north, on Herald Street, is the **Herald Street Caffè** (tel: 250 381 1441; Wed–Sun brunch), a good choice for lunch.

Returning along waterside Government Street, stop in at **Munro's Books** (No 1108, tel: 250 382 2464), one of Canada's finest bookstores, cross the street to the legendary **Rogers' Chocolates**, a Victorian institution for sweet tooths.

Top: Butchart Gardens

A Quarry Transformed

Visitors shouldn't leave Victoria without a trip to the **Butchart Gardens** (tel: 250 652 5256; daily from 9am, closing times vary depending on the season; admission charge). If you're travelling by bus, you will need to connect to the No 75 Central Saanich (Victoria Transit, tel: 250 382 6161).

Always full of euphoric gardeners, this series of gardens is based in a former quarry, which was transformed by the ambitious Jenny Butchart after her husband, Robert Pim Butchart, had extracted the limestone for his cement company. Since work began in 1904, this venerable garden has grown to 20 hectares (50 acres) of year-round blooms with over a million bedding plants rotated through different areas each season.

A tour usually starts with the first garden, in the floor of the quarry, which features classical statuary and a fountain among lush plantings. Proceed through the Rose Garden, Japanese Garden and Italian Garden, the latter occupying the former tennis court of the Butcharts' home. On some summer evenings the gardens are open late for musical and fireworks events. The only drawbacks are the strong sense of commercialism and surging crowds during the high-bloom and tourist season.

Breweries Trail

Victoria is known for its English heritage, from the elegant afternoon teas at the Empress Hotel to the fish-and-chip shops and the British-style pubs. As in the 'mother country', beer really matters, and this Anglo-Saxon city offers a six-pack of brewpubs. Even at the height of the tourist season, there are few things better than a 'hail, ale' tour along the **Victoria Brew Trail**. Stops (if you can manage them all) include **Buckerfields Brewery** (506 Pandora Avenue, tel: 250 361 3310) at the Swans Hotel, with its glass patio; the **Canoe Brewpub** (450 Swift Street, tel: 250 361 1940) at the Harbour Club; **Hugo's Grill & Brewhouse** (619 Courtney Street, tel: 250 920 4844); the **Lighthouse Brewery** (836 Devonshire Road, tel: 250 383 6500), for a factory-only tour. But if you prefer a tour with a beer store stop try the **Vancouver Island Brewery** (2330 Government Street, tel: 250 361 0005). The best place to eat and quaff the beer is **Spinnakers Brewpub** (308 Catherine Street, tel: 250 386 2739), which serves hearty dishes, including house-smoked sausages, on a waterfront deck. It's a great place for relaxing and meeting the locals. You can take the Brew Trail tour on your own or join a group, which means you don't have to drive. For group bookings, contact Colwood Travel (tel: 800 970 7722).

Visitors can stay overnight (or 'roll home' as the parlance goes) at a hostelry in the vicinity of the pubs. For the ultimate dining dream, head for **Sooke Harbour House** *(see page 71)* on Whiffen Spit Road. Located 22km (14 miles) west of Victoria overlooking the Strait of Juan de Fuca, the

Right: Sooke Harbour hosts

thoughtfully appointed lodge has been built around the sunlit restaurant, which has an international reputation and is consistently voted one of the top five restaurants in Canada. The chef uses the finest local fish, meat and vegetables seasoned with herbs from the gardens surrounding the house. If you can get a room here, you'd be advised to do so. It's best to arrive by cab from Victoria – expensive, but worth it. Alternatively, the **Swans Suite Hotel** (tel: 250 361-3310) has the roomiest digs, with some suites sleeping six, while **Spinnakers' Guesthouses B&B** (tel: 250 386 2739 or 877 838 2739), comprise three separate buildings set in heritage gardens, one of them a painstakingly restored 1884 home. Additional dining and late-night options in downtown Victoria include: the **Garlic Rose** *(see page 70)*, **Szechuan** *(see page 72)*, **Hunters** *(see page 75)* and **Pagliacci's** *(see page 70)*.

Pick up a copy of the free *Monday Magazine* for current information on cultural events and entertainment. On your return to Vancouver by plane try to secure port side seats again for a good look at Victoria, Vancouver Island, the Gulf Islands and the Coast Range.

2. GULF ISLANDS: GALIANO *(see map, p4)*

'The water is cool but can be quite pleasant on an incoming tide', reads the official guide for Galiano Island in the heart of Canada's Gulf Islands. Rural to wild and unquestionably beautiful, quaint with a touch of British rustic, the Gulf Islands are a refuge from Vancouver's urbanity. Served by frequent ferries, this string of 11 major islands and about 200 smaller ones is popular with visitors and locals alike.

Begin by booking overnight accommodation for Galiano Island through the Canadian Gulf Islands B&B Reservations Service (tel: 1 888 539 2930). Make dinner reservations at the Woodstone Country Inn (tel: 250 539 2022). Secure car ferry reservations from Tsawwassen to (and from) Galiano (Sturdies Bay) with BC Ferries (tel: 1 888 223 3779). You can also fly with West Coast Air (tel: 604 606 6888 or 604 299 9000 ext 6888). A floatplane will take you from downtown Vancouver to the Galiano Inn in 35 minutes.

Located across the Georgia Strait in the weather lee of Vancouver Island, the Gulf Islands have a Mediterranean-type climate of extended summers and dry winters – Galiano, favourably situated in a rainshadow, has an average of only 46cm (18 inches) of rain per year – making the island a great year-round destination.

Of the three central Gulf Islands, **Pender** and **Saltspring** are the most popular. Pender is known for its many beaches and delightful coves, while Saltspring, with its modern seaside resort, is the biggest and most developed and its downtown of **Ganges** has all the usual tourist amenities. Accommodation ranges from the expensive but highly recommended **Hastings House** (tel: 250 537 2362

Above: Galiano girl **Top Right:** seafood supper
Right: Montague Harbour

or 1 800 359 6279) on Saltspring Island, to campsites located in the **Ruckle Provincial Park**, bordering private farmland. But although these islands have more amenities (and are also accessible via the Tsawwassen ferry), they also have more people per square kilometre.

Our excursion will be to finger-shaped Galiano Island, the wilder, simpler choice. Renting a bike (**Galiano Bicycle Rental**, Burrill Road, tel: 250 539 9906) is an adventurous and fun way to get around the island. Hikers can walk almost the entire length of the east coast, or climb **Mount Sutil** (323m/1,059ft) or **Mount Galiano** (342m/1,122ft) for views of the mainland mountains. Try the beach that's the favourite of the locals – **Coon Bay**, at the island's northern tip.

An Island Tour

The Tsawwassen ferry terminal is located south of Vancouver on Highway 99 (take Granville Street south and follow signs to 'Ferries, US Border'). Turn west on Highway 17 to Tsawwassen Terminal. Allow enough time to arrive one hour early. The direct sailing is a morning one across the shipping lanes of the Georgia Strait and through the strong currents of Active Pass to **Sturdies Bay** (one of two ferry landing sites on Galiano.)

Driving off the ferry dock note the people: some local, some visitors. The 76-sq. km (29-sq. mile) island you are entering is home to no more than 1,000 year-round residents. Take the first left (cutting through the waiting off-island cars) and continue on the right to the **Visitor Information Booth** (tel: 250 539 2507; July–Aug: daily 8am–5pm) at 2590 Sturdies Bay

Road, which also provides bike, boat and canoe rentals. Stop here for a map of the island, then follow the road to the fork, taking a left on Montague Harbour Road to the centre of town.

On the left is the **Corner Store**; on the right is the **Day Star Market** (tel: 250 539 2800). Buy some picnic food for later then settle in for some tea, freshly baked goods, great salads and a closer look at the local people. Galiano is known for its potters, poets, artists and organic farmers – some of them hippies (and their descendants) who arrived here in 1960s. The **Galiano Art Gallery**, within the **Galiano Inn**, features local artworks, as does **Ixchel Crafts**, with outlets at Montague Marina (tel: 250 539 9819; mid-Apr to mid-Oct) and Georgeson Bay Road (tel: 250 539 3038; Fri–Sun.) The main political issues discussed on the island usually revolve around timber rights to this heavily forested land.

Parks and Beaches

On the road again follow the signs to **Montague Harbour Provincial Park** (tel: 250 391 2300), a marine reserve with two beaches, and providing visitors with a chance to do some fishing or dig for clams. 'When the tide goes out, the table is laid', Galiano pioneer Edward Winstnaley noted. The marina has a store and anchorage. In the park there are cycle-in, drive-in, walk-in and boat-in campsites. For information about camping here contact the BC Parks office (tel: 604 689 9025; 1 800 689 9025).

The white shell beach on the north side marks one of several middens (refuse heaps) that suggest First Nations occupation dating back over 3,000 years. Castaway shells left by centuries of shellfish harvesting formed berms. Constant wave action erodes the middens, crushes the shells and redeposits them to create Montague's white shell beaches. All this took place for thousands of years before Dionisio Galiano (1762–1805), a Spanish naval

Top: the Purple Caravan second-hand clothing store, Galiano

commander with the Malaspina expedition, explored the area in 1792. When he returned to Spain his writings disproved Juan de Fuca's Northwest Passage. Galiano bequeathed his surname to this island and gave his first name to another point on the island. At the end of the western point is a good spot to settle for a while – remember, this is a relaxing overnight stay. Keep an eye out for kingfishers, eagles, oyster-catchers, cormorants, harbour seals and leopard slugs, too.

Back on the main road turn right and head west (up island) on Porlier Pass Road for some excellent marine views. The northern tip of the island and **Dionisio Point Provincial Park** (tel: 250 391 2300), with its rocky headlands flanked by sandy beaches and picturesque bays, is accessible only by water. It has dramatic mature forests of Douglas fir, western hemlock, western red cedar and arbutus, and a tidal lagoon. To reach the park you will need to rent a 5-m (16-ft) motor boat at **Galiano Boat Rentals** (tel: 250 539 9828) in the Montague Harbour marina, or use the **Dionisio Point Park Water Taxi** (tel: 250 539 3109), which leaves from the Spanish Hills Wharf. Have your picnic lunch at **Dionisio Point**, with its sweeping views of Porlier Pass (currents up to 10 knots) and the northern Georgia Strait. Be careful not to trample the wildflowers (the little succulents are called stonecrop). If you have time why not visit two other beautiful parks in the area: **Bluff** and **Bellhouse**, easily accessible by car.

Staying Overnight

For good French cuisine the Wisteria Dining Room in the **Woodstone Country Inn**, at 743 Georgeson Bay Road is recommended for your evening meal. Turn left off Sturdies Road and follow the signs. The fixed-price, four-course dinner uses fresh island vegetables and fruits. The only competition is **La Berengerie** *(see page 75)*, a small genteel West Coast French restaurant on the corner of Montague and Clanton roads, or the reasonably priced **Hummingbird Inn**, at 47 Sturdies Bay Road, for pub food and local atmosphere. From the Woodstone you can stroll back beneath the stars to your lodgings and the morning ferry.

Overnight accommodation must be reserved in advance. At the **Galiano Inn** (134 Madrona Drive, tel: 250 539 3388), you'll find luxurious rooms overlooking Active Pass, Mayne Island and Washington's Olympic Mountains. For something simpler contact the **Sutil Lodge** (Montague Harbour, tel: 250 539 2930), a restored 1928 beachfront fishing lodge surrounded by acres of forest. This lodge offers an optional 4-hour nature cruise aboard a catamaran and a free ferry and canoe pick-up. An even more rugged choice on the island's quiet northern end are seven individual log cabins at **Bodega**

Right: a sailboat docked at Cain Bay

Resort (120 Monastee Road, off Porlier Pass Drive and Cook Drive, tel: 250 539 2677), with kitchens and wood-burning stoves. The accommodation is set in several hectares of forests and meadows with wonderful sea views.

3. NORTH TO WHISTLER *(see map, p4)*

Deep into the Coast mountains, a scenic fjord drive leads to one of the best international skiing and summer sports towns in North America, with outdoor activities that will suit all tastes at all times of the year. Selected as the site for the 2010 Winter Olympics, the Whistler Blackcomb resort is world class.

Plan to stay one to two nights. The winter season is mid-Nov–Apr. Summer (July–Sept) is best, although it can be chilly. Make bookings through Whistler Central Reservations (tel: 604 904 7060; 1 888 403 4727 [toll free]; International/UK, tel: 0800 731 5983 [toll free]). The Fairmont Chateau Whistler (tel: 604 938 8000; 1 800 606 8244 [toll free]), is among the finest of the big hotels, as is the Coast Whistler Hotel (tel: 604 932 2522; 1 800 663 5544 [toll free]). For dinner call Araxi (tel: 604 932 4540). Transport includes BC Rail (tel: 604 984 5246), which has a daily passenger service to and from Whistler. Perimeter Whistler Express (tel: 604 266 5386) has several daily bus departures from the Vancouver bus depot at 1150 Station Street. Alternatively you can book a flight through Whistler Air Services (tel: 604 932 6615). Almost everything in Whistler village is accessible on foot.

Thirty-five years ago the Whistler Valley consisted of a few fly-fishing lodges and isolated homesteads; there was no town, just an unpaved highway cutting beneath the high, glaciated mountains of the Coast Range. Today Whistler is a four-season resort with cobbled streets, more than 100 outdoor cafés, bistros and restaurants, a conference centre, more than 200 shops,

whistler excursion

and in excess of 5,000 guest rooms, ranging from a myriad of luxury condominiums, hotels and lodges to simple pensions and hostels. All this is located in a crisp alpine village setting that is an irresistibly attractive year-round destination, which has been described as 'Disneyland for Adults', by Vancouver writer, Steve Threndyle. **Whistler Mountain** and adjoining **Blackcomb Mountain** (often incorrectly lumped together as part of Whistler), have evolved into mountains with well-maintained summer and winter trails and all the amenities to go with them. The rich and famous visit in droves, so keep your eyes open.

On the Sea-to-Sky Highway

From downtown Vancouver start out early and plan for a two-hour drive (two-to three-hours in winter; it may also be lengthened by road improvement work preparing for the 2010 Winter Olympics) by crossing the Lions Gate Bridge to the North Shore, and following the signs for West Vancouver/Highway 99. Turn right on Taylor Way and then left (west) onto the four-lane Upper Levels Freeway. Approaching Horseshoe Bay, follow the signs to Squamish/Whistler. Passing Horseshoe Bay, one of the world's truly great highway-drives begins, full of drama and wild beauty.

Named the **Sea-to-Sky Highway**, Highway 99 climbs, dips and winds along the western edge of the North American continent, with sheer cliffs on **Howe Sound**, a true fjord representative of much of the 25,800-km (16,000-mile) coastline of British Columbia. At **Brittania Beach** you can visit the **British Columbia Museum of Mining** (tel: 1 800 896

4044, ext 227; May–mid-Oct: daily 9am–5.30pm; winter: Mon–Fri 9am–4.30pm; admission charge). Just short of Squamish, right off the highway, take a short stroll to **Shannon Falls**, at 340m (1,111ft) it is the third-highest waterfall in British Columbia. Further along is the **Stawamus Chief**, a 650-m (2,140-ft) high granite massif that attracts intrepid rock climbers.

North of Squamish, the aptly-named **Diamond Head** peak dominates the skyline to the east. This stark summit is the scooped-out remnant of Mount Garibaldi, an extinct volcano that forms part of the Pacific Rim ring of fire. Another volcanic remnant, the jagged **Black Tusk**, is visible further

Left: view to Whistler
Top: a mountain hike **Right:** heli skiing is a Whistler experience not to be missed

north. Both areas are located in **Garibaldi Provincial Park** (tel: 604 898 3678), an area with extensive hiking trails.

The Number One Resort

The officially named **Resort Municipality of Whistler** (Tourism Whistler: 4010 Whistler Way, tel: 604 938 2769) is the only town in Canada actually founded as a resort. Famous for excellent lift systems the Whistler and Blackcomb mountains are rated number one in North America by ski and snowboard aficionados. You can ski through July high on **Blackcomb's Horstman Glacier**. Call 604 932 3434 or 1 800 766 0449 (toll free) for ski information and updates; tel: 604 938 7737 for snowboard rentals.

Thirty-three lifts run from November to July, providing more than 1.3 million skier days per year. Whistler and Blackcomb have 200 trails to challenge all ability levels, not to mention three glaciers – two of which

are 1.6km (1 mile) high – legendary bowls, trail skiing and some of the hairiest chutes and couloirs in the West. The Whistler Blackcomb resort has more than 2,833 hectares (7,000 acres) compared to Aspen's 273 hectares (675 acres), and Whistler trumps the field with the two longest vertical drops on the continent – 1,609m (5,280 ft) on Blackcomb and 1,530m (5,020ft) on Whistler Mountain. Here too you can ski nearly 11km (7 miles) from top to bottom – if your thighs can stand it.

Each mountain deserves a full day. Surprisingly, the Whistler Blackcomb summer is its winter's equal. There's a plethora of year-round outdoor activities, with guides and equipment rentals on hand. You can play golf, hike the mountain trails, swim, paraglide, roller blade, canoe, kayak, sail, river-raft, jet-boat, windsurf, fly-fish, horse ride, rock climb, hot-air balloon and play tennis. If you want to mountain bike – the extreme way – reserve gear at Whistler Eco Tours Ltd (4220 Gateway Boulevard, tel: 604 935 4900) and take a guided gondola lift up to the top for an exhilarating, don't-hit-your-front-brakes ride down.

Whether you have been careening down the **Whistler Mountain Bike Park** at high speeds or leisurely pedalling the gentle grades of the **Valley Trail**, you can take a break and catch one of Whistler's public buses, which have bike racks on the front so that they can accommodate weary cyclists.

To book any Whistler outdoor activity from heli-rafting to Hummer tours, call the **Whistler Activity Centre** (tel: 604 938 2769; 1 877 991 9988; open daily 9am–5pm). And for a day away from the crowds you can try helicopter skiing (Whistler Heli-Skiing, tel: 604 932 4105). Be warned, it's not an inexpensive activity and all participants must be strong intermediate skiers. The tour company will provide the transport and lunch. If you visit in winter a favourite activity, not to be missed, is a nighttime snowmobile ride on wooded trails under December's full moon.

Above: there's fun for everyone at Whistler

Winter or summer, even with absolutely no skiing ability, you can have fun. Ride the gondola (or 'quad') chairs to the mountaintops and enjoy the Coast Range view over lunch on the veranda at any of Blackcomb's mountainside restaurants. Try the rustic **Horstman Hut** *(see page 69)*, located at the top of the Seventh Heaven Express chair, perched at 2,284m (7,494ft), for simple chilli, hearty stew or macaroni and cheese. On sunny days you can enjoy a smoky barbecue on what appears to be the top of the world, with spectacular views of the entire valley. Back in the resort, try **Ingrid's Village Café** (tel: 604 932 7000), a deli at Skiers Plaza, or a long-standing favourite Italian restaurant well-known for its impeccable lunch and dinner creations, the upmarket **Il Caminetto Di Umberto** *(see page 70)*.

A Walk in the Woods

Be sure to take a stroll through the pedestrian-only village streets filled with alluring shops stocked with expensive skiwear. There is a short wooded walk between Whistler village and Blackcomb's (just-as-tastefully done)

village. Enjoy the heather- and hemlock-scented air while you wonder just how sore your muscles will be tomorrow.

There is a summer-long calender of music festivals – including classical, country and blues – summer theatre, photography workshops and even the occasional Saturday-night star-gazing event from the top of Blackcomb Mountain (using portable telescopes from the Vancouver Planetarium).

Top: skiing on Blackcomb
Left: young blades

Leisure Activities

SHOPPING

Vancouver is great for people who rarely shop because here it can be a cultural as well as a commercial experience. The high quality, range of tastes, strong European roots, outstanding First Nations art and imaginative home-grown talent shows in window after shop window. There is a strong single-owner ethic here that strives for the unique item that you won't find in a chain store (and there are fewer of these in Vancouver). Best of all, a vibrant, relatively young and affluent inner-city community supports this creativity. Equally important is price. Canada generally keeps its dollar low compared to the rest of the Commonwealth and the US dollar, and goods generally cost 15–30 percent less, depending on the currency). You can also apply for a Goods and Services Tax (GST) refund on departure (*see Practical Information, page 86*).

Vancouver has its department stores and its shopping malls but the most interesting discoveries are in the older shopping districts, where retailers tend to be both discriminating and exuberant. Here you'll find shopping enclaves specializing in a particular type of merchandise. Detailed below are some of the high, hot and odd spots.

Robson Street

Also known as 'Robsonstrasse' this is where you'll find eclectic, designer clothing, notably in the three blocks between **Burrard** and **Bute** streets. It's the closest thing Vancouver has to an exclusive enclave, and with the exception of weekday evenings in winter, Robson Street is crammed with people.Try one of many trendy outlets such as **Emile Klein** (1285 Robson Street, tel: 604 608 4242) for men's and women's fashions. If you love shoes, local footwear architect **Stéphane de Raucourt** (1067 Robson Street, tel: 604 681 8814) designs unique styles you won't see anywhere else.

The sharpest fashion shoppers venture just a bit further afield. Away from Robson's high rents and high traffic, boutiques such as Chanel, Louis Vuitton, Celine, Fendi and Prada congregate in the so-called **International Zone** near Robson on **Burrard** and **Hornby** streets. You can create your own jewellery design or choose from a sexy assortment in sterling or 14-carat gold at **Van Ny** in **Style Design Gallery** (969 Hornby Street, tel: 604 315 2137).

If it's raining there's an entire mall hidden underground. **Pacific Centre** on the corner of West Georgia and Howe streets (tel: 604 688 7235) has nearly 200 flashy stores, a large food fair and access to **Sears**, **The Bay** and **Holt Renfrew** department stores.

Granville Street

Across False Creek, the Fairview district has a smattering of fashion retailers, plus an assortment of fine arts and antiques dealers. This neighbourhood has also long been an enclave for Asian rug dealers. Stop off at **Spirits of the North** (2327 Granville Street, tel: 604 733 8516), a gallery for West Coast tribal art. Or you can visit the **Diane Farris Gallery** (1565 West 7th Avenue, tel: 604 737 2629), an institution that has boosted several local artists to international stardom. Two internationally renowned designers also do business here: the 'by appointment only' **Zonda Nellis Designs** (2203 Granville Street, tel: 604 736 5668), features hand-woven separates and hand-painted cut velvets for women, and **Martha Sturdy** (3039 Granville Street, tel: 604 737 7822), who is known for her poured resin bowls, clunky jewellery and home accessories. Classic women's fashions can be found at **Edward Chapman and Circa-ici** (2596 Granville Street, tel: 604 732 1958), plus

Left: shop at the Old House and Home
Right: Government Street banner

an in-store showcase for local designers. Across the street is the trendy **Restoration Hardware** (2555 Granville Street, tel: 604 731 3918), which stocks stylish homeware, and a few blocks away is **Yumi Eto** (No 305, 1008 Homer Street, tel: 604 689 8320), with beautiful women's designs blending European and Japanese style.

The store on the corner of Granville Street and West 75th Street that looks like a Pacific Northwest longhouse is **Dorothy Grant Ltd** (1656 West 75th Street, tel: 604 681 0201), here the designer exhibits her unique First Nations designs as well as a collection of exquisitely detailed Haida motifs by her husband, acclaimed artist Robert Davidson. These she appliqués onto coats, leather vests, jackets, caps and accessories. The clothes are gorgeous and she also stocks contemporary Haida art and jewellery.

Camperland

Vancouver is so close to a vast wilderness it's no surprise that its nature lovers need both appropriate apparel and rugged supplies. The resulting agglomeration of merchants is so-called 'Camperland', just east of Granville Street – a district specializing in the great outdoors. More than a dozen stores between Eighth and Broadway and cross-streets Yukon and Ontario are dedicated to Vancouverites' love affair with rock-climbing, hiking, skiing, kayaking and camping. The **Mountain Equipment Co-op** (130 West Broadway, tel: 604 876 6221) is the biggest, while **Taiga Works** (390 West Broadway, tel: 604 875 6644) has a good selection of Gore-Tex jackets and puffy vests that can withstand the cold Canadian temperatures in the winter.

Granville Island

Trendy Granville Island (tel: 604 666 5784) is a fascinating mix of art and crafts, household and kitchen goods and a superb food market. Top attractions include the intimate collection of speciality stores at the **Net Loft**, including **Paper-Ya** (No 9, 1666 Johnston Street, tel: 604 684 2531) which stocks exquisite handmade writing papers. Nearby, **The Crafthouse** (1386 Cartwright Street, tel: 604 687 7270), is a showcase for functional (rather than merely decorative) work by Canadian artists.

Gastown

Victorian street lamps line the cobblestone streets of the historic district where Vancouver began. Classy **Leone** (Sinclair Centre, 757 W Hastings Street, tel: 604 68. 1133), on the west side of Gastown, is modelled on an Italian streetscape and configured into exclusive designer boutiques. Along both sides of Water Street near the cruise ship dock, at Canada Place to Maple Tree Square, souvenir shops, galleries and restaurants occupy restored warehouses and refurbished 19th-century alleyways. Goods range from tacky tee-shirts to sweaters and handmade pottery, First Nations crafts and costume jewellery. A collection of crisp, modern furnishings is the attraction at **Inform** (97 Water Street, tel: 604 682 3868), while the **Inuit Gallery** (345 Water Street, tel: 604 688 7323) has a superb array of aboriginal art. Not too far off the beaten path is the venerable **Vancouver Pen Shop Ltd** (512 West Hastings Street, tel: 681 1612).

Kitsilano District

In the 1960s the 'Kits' neighbourhood was the student mecca. Today's residents are still on the edge of the counter-culture but their houses are worth $800,000 or more. Hoardings here show murals of people exercising, eating well and pampering themselves. There are multitudes of places on West First and West Fourth avenues, West Broadway and West Tenth Avenue marketing this lifestyle, and the hippie health-food shops of the 1960s have long since gone upmarket. Yorkville, named for its proximity to York Street on the 1800-block of West 1st Avenue, epitomizes this so perfectly it almost feels like a movie set.

The 1700-block of West Fourth Avenue is a mecca for board sports – snow, skim, wake, surf and skate – and sponsored athletes and their groupies gather here. Some of the best locally designed skate and streetwear can be found here at **Thriller** (No 1710), and **Pacific Boarder** (No 1793, tel: 604 734 7245), and **Westbeach** (No 1766, tel: 604 731 6449), almost as famous in Japan and Germany as it is in Canada. Westbeach sells every kind of sports board, produces its own technical streetwear, and hosts skateboarding demos in the back of the store.

Drinkwater and Company (4465 West 10th Avenue, tel: 604 224 2665) is a family-operated kitchen store carrying linen tea towels, French utensils and imported ceramics. It looks modest, but some of the city's top chefs shop here.

Yaletown

Ten years ago, Yaletown, along Mainland Street, was little more than a dilapidated cluster of old warehouses, but now these addresses are the trendiest in town with restaurants, funky pubs, artists' lofts, furniture dealers and high fashion clothing and shoe stores. Favoured by models and stylists, **Atomic Model Boutique** (1036 Mainland Street, tel: 604 688 9989) stocks designer-diffusion lines ahead of other stores. Jason Matlo is definitely a fashion label to seek out, available at **Vasanji** (1012 Mainland Street, tel: 604 669 0882). **Don't Show The Elephant** (1207 Hamilton Street, tel: 604 331 1018), home of custom-designed

furniture and blown-glass Japanese ice-coffee makers, is a gallery cum café while elegant furniture and accoutrements are sourced from around the world at **Liberty Design** (1295 Seymour Street, tel: 604 682 7499). Lines don't get much cleaner than those at **Living Space Interiors** (1110 Mainland Street, tel: 604 683 1116), with its Italian and French furniture and home accessories.

Funnily enough, the **Commercial Drive** area is not so much for shopping as for having a look-and-see experience. 'The Drive', as it's known locally, stretches from Venables Street to East Tenth Avenue and exudes a way of life in which 1960s hippy idealism meets 1990s urban angst with a dash of old world Italy (its nickname 'Little Italy' is now rather dated). You won't find designer labels, but you will see people wearing the most spirited styles in the city. You'll see hemp-fabric creations at every turn – dress the part and you just may be invited to a spontaneous didgeridoo jam at Grandview Park or, further afield, on the banks of Trout Lake, with its legendary **Farmers' Market** (3350 Victoria Drive, tel: 604 879 3276; Sat mornings mid-May–Oct). **Dr Vigari Gallery** – read it again, it's not a misprint – at 1312 Commercial Drive (tel: 604 255 9513) is a showcase of groovy furniture accessories, and **Mecca** (1204 Commercial Drive, tel: 604 251 7390) the place to go if you like ABW (Already Been Worn) clothes.

Antiques Row

Main Street between 16th and 25th Avenues is Antiques Row, with a broad assortment of traditional antiques and 20th-century nostalgia. Browsers clog the stores, especially on Sunday afternoons, and maze-like corridors have antiques stacked to the ceiling. Try **Deeler's Antiques** (4391 Main Street, tel: 604 879 3394), **Legends** (4366 Main Street, tel: 604 875 0621), with its vintage rhinestone jewellery and 'Jackie O' pillboxes. For fashions with character and intriguing accessories, head for central Main Street, home of **Eugene Choo** (No 3683), where Canadian designer women's wear hangs alongside international labels, ultra-feminine **Barefoot Contessa** (No 3715), and innovative **Front & Co**. (No 3772).

Left: a colourful stand in Gastown

EATING OUT

The 'unrepentant exuberance of the west coast', a quote from *Where to Eat in Canada*, sums up the adventure of dining in Vancouver. With more than 2,000 restaurant, there are legions of good restaurants chasing many great ones. The energy is everywhere – in the neighbourhoods, in the ethnic business districts, the bustling downtown core, the rural inns. Even the hotels, usually bastions of the status quo, are attentive and ambitious.

What works foodwise in Vancouver? A mix of ingredients – Northwest greens, salmon and shellfish – influences from California, the Southwest, Europe and Asia fuse to form Vancouver's enviable cuisine. BC wines keep winning international awards but are expensive, while the city's sushi bars are the best and lowest priced in Canada.

The list that follows is just a sampler, starting with restaurants with a view, then following roughly in order of the most popular cuisines that locals prefer, headed up by Italian. All recommended restaurants are more or less within the central areas covered in this book. The listings illustrate the range and ingenuity of the chefs as well as the cuisines of Vancouver, and definitions of each cuisine, as it's understood in Vancouver, are included. Note that prices quoted are in Canadian dollars and include a meal for one person with wine.

$= $5–$30
$$= $30–$60
$$$= More than $60

Dining with a View

Vancouver has a magnificent setting, and dining with a view includes gazing at the North shore mountains and the sea, looking out over a marina or enjoying a bird's-eye view of it all from the mountains – but there' a price to pay for all this. When you phone for a reservation specify your desire for a prime viewing spot – not all tables have one

Altitudes Bistro
6400 Nancy Greene Way, North Vancouver
Tel: 604 998 4398
A two-tiered patio atop Grouse Mountain offers a stunning view of the city; the house specialities include salmon fillet. $$$

Bridges
1696 Duranleau Street, Granville Island
Tel: 604 687 4400
A casual wharf-side patio overlooks boat-filled waters; inside is a vaulted upstairs dining room and a fresh seafood menu. $$$

Cardero's
1583 Coal Harbour Quay
Tel: 604 669 7666
Casual waterfront bar, dining room and patio with spectacular marina and mountain views. Specialises in seafood. $$$

Cloud 9 Revolving Restaurant
Empire Landmark Hotel, 1400 Robson Street
Tel: 604 662 8328
The food is hardly revolutionary, but the 42-

Top: dining al fresco on Granville Island

storey high panorama (complete circuit takes one hour) compensates. Drink well, eat light, and if you roam, don't lose your table. **$$$**

Horstman Hut
Blackcomb Mountain, top of 7th Heaven Express chair
High on the mountainside, with spectacular views; simple hearty fare, such as chilli or stew; barbecues in good weather. **$**

Imperial Chinese Seafood
Marine Building, 355 Burrard Street
Tel: 604 688 8191
This opulent, spacious restaurant commands a Burrard Inlet view and wows visitors with its Cantonese offerings and *dim sum* . **$$$**

Monk McQueen's or McQueen's Upstairs
601 Stamps Landing
Tel: 604 877 1351
Extensive waterside patio on False Creek with sweeping views of downtown and the North Shore mountains. It has an oyster bar, fresh seafood, pasta and grills. Upstairs is more elegant; live jazz at weekends. **$$$**

The Five Sails
Pan Pacific Hotel, 999 Canada Place Way
Tel: 604 662 8111
Arguably the finest of all view dining rooms within the heart of downtown, where choices may include poached oysters followed by grilled ahi tuna with a wasabi-potato napoleon for a main course, all presented with seamless service. **$$$**

Salmon House on the Hill
2229 Folkestone Way, West Vancouver
Tel: 604 926 3212
Perennial favourite, with – not surprisingly – grilled salmon as the speciality. First Nations decor combines with a panoramic view of downtown and Point Grey. **$$$**

Seasons in the Park
Queen Elizabeth Park
Tel: 604 874 8008
Ask for a window seat in this expansive room, or eat on the patio, to enjoy one of the best garden, neighbourhood and skyline views in the city. Solid service and a good wine list. **$$$**

Teahouse Restaurant
Ferguson Point, Stanley Park
Tel: 604 669 3281
Natural light, old wood, white linen and contemporary menu. Good views from the two atriums, or you can eat outside. **$–$$**

Italian and Mediterranean

Popular styles reflect several Italian regions, but such Americanised dishes as ravioli, lasagne or spaghetti with meatballs are rare. Far more popular are antipastis, including bruschettas, rich Tuscan soups, home-made pasta combinations, mortadella, calzones, thin-crust pizzas, veal and duck dishes.

Allegro Café
888 Nelson Street
Tel: 604 683 8485
Warm sophisticated setting with pasta dishes and Italian flavours to match, on the ground floor of a modest office building. **$$**

Amercord
1168 Hamilton Street
Tel: 604 681 6500
Dishes from the Bologna and Emilia Romagna areas of Italy are elegantly presented with clear, natural flavours. **$$**

Bacchus Ristorante
Wedgewood Hotel, 845 Hornby Street
Tel: 604 689 7777 or 1 800 663 0666
Award-winning restaurant, with Nova Scotia lobster, Fraser Valley duck and Alberta beef as the basis of creative dishes. **$$**

Ciao Bella Ristorante Italiano
703 Denman Street
Tel: 604 688 5771
Elegant decor, courteous service, authentic Italian cuisine and a romantic atmosphere. Hundreds of pasta combinations are on offer, or veal, chicken, seafood and vegetarian dishes. **$$$**

CinCin Italian Wood Grill
1154 Robson Street
Tel: 604 688 7338
Warm terracotta and wood smoke sets the scene for Tuscan-Mediterranean dishes. Between meals the bar is open for antipasti and pizza. Reservations advised. **$$$**

Cioppino's Mediterranean Grill & Enoteca
1129–1133 Hamilton Street
Tel: 604 688 7466
'Best Italian' in *Vancouver* magazine 2004, the menu here might feature sea bass casserole with artichokes, or chanterelles and white kidney beans. Formal grill and more casual enoteca. **$$$**

Garlic Rose
1205 Wharf Street, Victoria
Tel: 250 384 1962
Seafood platters are served Mediterranean-style, with a wide choice of pastas; view of harbour from the patio.

Il Caminetto Di Umberto
Whistler Village
Tel: 604 932 4442
Impeccable food and service, plus a long wine list, makes this a memorable restaurant.

Il Giardino di Umberto
1382 Hornby Street
Tel: 604 669 2422
Dine al fresco on the a romantic, vine-draped terrace or by candlelight in an elegant dining room. Umberto creates Tuscan flavours and offers a superior wine list. **$$$**

Pagliacci's
1011 Broad Street, Victoria
Tel: 250 386 1011
Southern Italian food, including good pizza and cheesecake. Lively atmosphere, with easy-listening jazz and other live music some evenings. **$–$$**

Romano's Macaroni Grill
1523 Davie Street
Tel: 604 689 4334
Authentic Italian food is served up in this stunning heritage mansion. The atmosphere is casual, with impromptu arias from waiters. Menu includes *paesano* (family) dinners. **$$**

West Coast Cuisine
West Coast cuisine seeks out the freshest local ingredients, prepares them with a marked interest in a 'fusion' of various cooking styles, and attention to the region's health-conscious traditions. Offerings tend to be fresh, crisp, crunchy and lean. Specialities include fresh fish, berries, mushrooms, white asparagus, Chinese vegetables, a few local cheeses and many British Columbia wines from the Okanagan Valley.

Cru
1459 West Broadway
Tel: 604 677 4111
This restaurant has an urban-modern decor and an intimate wine bar. Small plates or a four-course prix fixe blur the line between fine dining and bistro. **$$**

Diva at the Met
Metropolitan Hotel, 645 Howe Street
Tel: 604 602 7788
Gourmet magazine calls this Vancouver's best restaurant. The menu presents gorgeously arranged food with an emphasis on the Pacific Northwest; great brunch too. **$$$**

Fiddlehead Joe's
No 1A, 1012 Beach Avenue
Tel: 604 688 1969
A picturesque spot on the seawall, with a seasonal menu that usually includes rack of lamb, curried cream mussels, sockeye salmon and fiddleheads (young ferns). **$$**

Griffins
Fairmont Hotel, 900 W Georgia Street
Tel: 604 684 3131
Bright and vibrant brasserie that frequently tops the best restaurant polls. Superb buffet, plus a la carte. Smart casual dress. **$$**

Pair Bistro
3763 West 10th Avenue
Tel: 604 224 7211
First Nations artwork sets the scene for regional cuisine such as local sturgeon or seafood cioppino. The wine list features only British Columbia wines. **$$**

Raincity Grill
1193 Denman Street
Tel: 604 685 7337
Modern, casually elegant place by English Bay, which defines West Coast cuisine with grilled foods based on absolutely fresh local ingredients and wines by the glass. **$$$**

Shaughnessy
Oak Street and 37th Avenue
Tel: 604 261 0011
At the entrance to the VanDusen Botanical Garden, a light and airy restaurant with natural wood, slate and plants. Heated outdoor deck for year-round dining amid exotic plants. Innovative contemporary cuisine. **$$**

Sooke Harbour House
1528 Whiffen Spit Road, Sooke
Tel: 250 642 3421
Consistently among the top five restaurants in Canada. The finest local fish, meat and vegetables are used, with herbs from the kitchen garden, in creative concoctions. **$$$**

West
2881 Granville Street
Tel: 604 738 8938
A local champion of British Columbia cuisine; seasonal ingredients are prepared with unswerving techniques. **$$$**

Chinese

Authentic Chinese cuisine here reflects specific Chinese provinces or cities and come chopstick-ready (chopped). North American 'Chinese food' – chow mein, chop suey, egg foo yong and fortune cookies – while found here, is not considered noteworthy. Instead there is a drill down of knowledge about China. Cantonese food, which most Westerners know best, is decidedly mild, noted for its slow cooked soups, or quickly assembled melanges with seafood or white meats and bean sprouts with soy sauce, ginger, garlic and spring onion. It also includes a local favourite, *dim sum*, meaning 'a little meal to touch the heart'. Three other styles are prominent: Szechuan, noted for beef and hot chilli spiciness; Shanghai, featuring stir-fried dishes prepared with oil, ginger, sugar and wine, but little spiciness; and Mandarin, reputedly originating from the Emperor's kitchens in Beijing – a fusion of other styles.

Beijing Restaurant
865 Hornby Street
Tel: 604 688 7788
This place specialises in seafood dishes prepared in the style of Cantonese, Szechuan and Shanghai cuisine. **$$**

Right: a tempting sign

Hon's Wun Tun House
1339 Robson Street
Tel: 604 688 0871
Decades-old Chinatown favourite offering noodles and simmered potstickers. It's crowded, noisy and fun; the menu features 90 soups and vegetarian *dim sum*. **$**

Landmark Hotpot House
4023 Cambie Street
Tel 604 872 2868
If you don't mind your dinner wriggling, try the sashimi selection. Otherwise, start with the dual soup base and add the heaping seafood-combination. Picture-perfect presentation and fresh ingredients. **$$**

Park Lock Seafood Restaurant
544 Main Street (upstairs)
Tel: 604 688 1581
Great place for *dim sum* with meat, seafood or vegetable fillings. **$$**

Pink Pearl Chinese Seafood Restaurant
1132 East Hastings Street
Tel: 604 253 4316
This classic Chinese restaurant offers dozens of simple, old-fashioned Cantonese dishes from an easy-to-read menu, with exceptional *dim sum* and fresh seafood in its live tanks. Portions are unusually large. **$$**

Shanghai Chinese Bistro
1124 Alberni Street
Tel: 604 683 8222
Shanghai and Szechuan menus are in English,

Chinese and Japanese. Fresh seafood is a speciality, with hand-pulled noodles and chilli wontons, plus daily specials and *dim sum*. **$$**

Szechuan Chongqing
2808 Commercial Drive
Tel: 604 254 7434
A must for those who love their Szechuan dishes to range from blasting hot to seriously fiery to incendiary, the usual favourites here include spicy green beans. **$$**

Szechuan Exotic Chinese Cuisine
853 Caledonia Avenue, Victoria
Tel: 250 384 0224
The best place in Victoria for fresh seafood and Chinese cuisine; long menu, plus take-away option. **$**

Toko
223 West 7th Avenue
Tel: 604 879 0701
Oodles of noodles in the Chinese, Japanese or Korean traditions at this pan-Asian restaurant-cum-noodle factory. Other favourites include hot-and-sour soup and peanut-based tan tan noodles. **$**

Japanese

Excellence in Japanese cuisine, as defined in Vancouver, includes various types of sushi and sashimis – bite-sized morsels made with raw fish (especially salmon and tuna) or shellfish. Because they must be served absolutely fresh, the restaurants employ well-trained knife-welding chefs who do nothing else. Miso soup is a staple as is green tea. Tempura refers to deep fried battered seafood and vegetables. Lunchtime restaurants offer *bento* (a boxed meal). Vancouver rivals the great cities of Japan both for authenticity, quality and price.

Ajisai Sushi Bar
2081 West 42nd Avenue
Tel: 604 266 1428
Wall-to-wall sushi and sashimi, this tucked-away Kerrisdale gathering place dishes out thoughtfully prepared classics that sing. **$**

Guu With Garlic
1698 Robson Street
Tel: 604 685 8678
Homesick Japanese students rub shoulders with globally minded hipsters here. Daily specials like marinated octopus or egg with pumpkin and mayonnaise represent Japanese fast food at its best. **$**

Gyu Japanese Teppanaki
219–755 Burrard Street
Tel: 604 688 7050
A casual spot where chefs put on quite a show preparing prawns, scallops, squid or filet mignon. Children's menu, too. **$$**

Gyoza King
1508 Robson Street
Tel: 604 669 8278
Dark-walled and funky, this little spot is a mega-happening haunt for Japanese locals. It's open late, and *gyozas* (fried pork or vege-table dumplings) reign supreme. **$**

Kakoemnon
200 Burrard Street, entrance off Cordova
Tel: 604 688 6866
An elegant sushi bar with private *tatami* rooms and a main restaurant. Ocean and mountain views provide the backdrop. **$$**

Kibune Sushi
1508 Yew Street
Tel: 604 731 4482
Long-established restaurant serving authentic Japanese cuisine; very good sushi.

Shijo
1926 West 4th Avenue
Tel: 604 732 4676
In a minimalist setting, imaginative dishes with finely tuned flavours include first-rate

Left: Nouveau but nice

sushi and sashimi, sunomono salad, miso oysters and gyoza. **$$**

Shiru-Bay Chopsticks Café
1193 Hamilton Street
Tel: 604 408 9315
This restaurant combines a great atmosphere with intriguing *izakaya* food, minimalist Japanese pub-style food on small plates. Portions would not constitute a full meal. **$**

Tojo's
777 West Broadway
Tel: 604 872 8050
The city and mountain views vie with visiting film stars for your attention as you nibble on parchment-baked sablefish or inside-out spicy-tuna rolls. Try ignoring the menu and say *Omakase* (let the chef decide). Rude waiters here often raise eyebrows. **$$$**

Greek

Though Greek immigration has been relatively modest, there is a plethora of Greek restaurants serving breaded calamari (squid), tzatziki (yoghurt with cucumber and garlic), hummus (chickpea dip) and dolmades (vine leaves stuffed either with meat or rice). Menus also feature moussaka (aubergine/eggplant casserole) and souvlaki (lamb and vegetables on skewers), and some specialise in *gyros* (meat, yoghurt and tomato on pita bread). Baklava desserts are also popular.

Anatoli Souvlaki
5 Lonsdale Avenue
Tel: 604 985 9853
Authentic Greek cuisine and atmosphere; pleasant patio to the rear.

Apollonia Restaurant
1839 1st Street
Tel: 604 746 9559
Home-style Cretan food in a warm, rustic, family-owned restaurant. Favourites include calamari and slow-roasted lamb. **$$**

Bouzyo's The Green Taverna
1815 Commercial Drive
Tel: 604 254 2533
This family-oriented restaurant boasts a large outdoor patio, nightly entertainment and generous sharing-platters. **$$**

Kalamata Greek Taverna
478 West Broadway
Tel: 604 872 7050
Inspired by southern Greek home cooking; tender roast lamb and calamari come with the best Greek salad in town. **$$**

Kalypso Restaurant
No 200, 1025 Robson Street
Tel: 604 689 5550
In the heart of downtown, with a huge patio overlooking Robson street, this place has great souvlaki, calamari, oven-roasted lamb and belly dancing (weekends only) **$$**

Romios Greek Taverna
2272 West 4th Avenue
Tel: 604 736 2118
Cosy, family-owned place; does a good lamb shank. **$**

Stepho's Souvlaki
1124 Davie Street
Tel: 604 683 2555
This is one of the city's best dining bargains, so you'll probably have to queue. Huge quantities of roast potatoes, souvlaki, calamari or steamed clams. **$**

Indian

Vancouver has a large and active East Indian population, and they have established dozens of notable restaurants. Celebrated for artful and aromatic combinations of spices, India celebrates all food as a sort of spiritual fuel for the human fire. Dishes well represented here include chapathi, curries, tandoori (clay oven) chicken and hot vindaloo.

A Taste of India
1282 Robson Street
Tel: 604 682 3894
This casual bistro specialises in tandoori, curried seafood, meat and vegetarian dishes. Dine in or take out. **$$**

Chutney Villa
147 East Broadway
Tel: 604 872 2228
South Indian cuisine, spicier but not as rich as food from more northerly areas, is served here, including dosas, idli and vadas. Dishes mainly based on rice and lentils. **$$**

Clove Café and Record Bar
2054 Commercial Drive
Tel: 604 255 5550
Funky alternative restaurant with Indian-influenced music and traditional Punjabi kitchen dishes such as subji, dahl, murgha and parantha, served on small plates.$

Maurya
1643 West Broadway
Tel: 604 742 0622
Flavourful plates ranging from butter chicken with fenugreek to fiery lamb vindaloo are served against the polished backdrop of luxurious decor. All spices are sourced in India. $$

Rubina Tandoori
1962 Kingsway
Tel: 604 874 3621
Serving the *lazeez* (delicious) cuisine of India, this is Canada's first 'heart smart' Indian Restaurant. Classic chicken, beef and lamb dishes are spiced with the likes of anise, cardamom, clove and cinnamon. $$

Sitar Indian Restaurant
8 Powell Street, Gastown
Tel: 604 687 0049
Colonising a colonnade in Gastown in an attractive setting of wood, brick and Indian-rug-draped-walls, you will find tandoori and tikkas, vindaloo, biriyani and korma as well as vegetarian choices. $$

Seafood
West Coast fish and shellfish is superlative, from the succulent Alaskan king crabs to salmon from local rivers, and the fine chefs of Vancouver know exactly what to do with it, either cooking it simply, as First Nations people have done for centuries, or creating exciting new recipes with fusion cuisine.

C Restaurant
1600 Howe Street
Tel: 604 681 1164
This consistently good restaurant is located on the downtown side of the False Creek seawall. Serving creative seafood dishes in a maritime setting, its specialities are seafood tartare and sashimi. $$$

Coast Restaurant
1257 Hamilton Street
Tel: 604 685 5010
A loft-style restaurant with contemporary, Zen-inspired decor. The menu offers Copper River salmon from Alaska, orange roughy from Australia, Spanish escolar, Chilean sea bass, sturgeon from the Caspian Sea and New Zealand swordfish. $$$

The Fish House
8901 Stanley Park Drive
Tel: 604 681 7275
In a charming renovated house overlooking putting greens and English Bay. Signature dishes include tiger prawns sautéed with garlic, roasted red peppers, tomatoes and feta cheese flambéed with ouzo. $$$

Joe Fortes Seafood and Chop House
777 Thurlow Street at Robson
Tel: 604 669 1940
San Francisco-style chophouse with an oyster bar. Sunbathe or sit in the shade among the foliage of the roof garden with its own grill. Live piano music nightly. $$$

Troll's
6408 Bay Street
Tel: 604 921 7755
Good fish and chips, overlooking Horseshoe Bay's busy harbour. $

American
Since the late 1960s, when a former Prime Minister compared Canada's cultural proximity to the United States as 'sleeping with an elephant', the influence of American entertainment and cuisine on the Canadian consciousness has not lessened one tiny bit. And while its details may be subject to disagreement, American cuisine at its most basic revolves around a 'good hunk a' meat' Western Canadians, and indeed visitors, who

Right: a healthy alternative for Saturday night drinks

feel like a good steak will find some 'good ol' boy' choices.

Bogart's Chophouse and Bar
1619 West Broadway
Tel: 604 733 4141
While the focus is on the meat, this restaurant also features seafood, pasta dishes, tapas – and live jazz. Go for the bison stew served with lager mushroom ragout. **$$**

Hunters
759 Yates Street, Victoria
Tel: 250 384 7494
Great mesquite-grilled steaks and tapas, with a long list of wines by the glass and beers on tap. Interesting artworks and decor.

Hy's Steakhouse
537 Hornby Strett
Tel: 604 683 7671
A favourite for more than 40 years, this is Vancouver's preeminent steak restaurant. Both lunch and dinner menus feature perfectly aged, charcoal broiled beefsteaks. Reservations suggested. **$$$**

Moderne Burger
2507 West Broadway,
Tel: 604 739 000
This 1940s-style burger joint has authentic retro-decor. Sirloin burgers are made from scratch, with veggie, turkey and salmon options available. **$** (cash only)

Sophie's Cosmic Café
2095 West 4th Avenue
Tel: 604 732 6810
It's worth the queue to get into this trendy place, great for families. All-day menu of interesting choices. Try the café's own cajun hot sauce. **$**

Tony Roma's Famous For Ribs
801 Pacific Street
Tel: 604 669 7336
A feast of slathered-in-sauce grilled ribs, judged to be the best in North America. Enjoy them in a relaxed dining room, takeaway or get delivery to your hotel room. **$$**

Wilson's Steak House
808 Beatty Street
Tel: 604 696 6787
Enjoy a good hunk of steak with style near BC Place. All meats are Canadian prime cuts and range from a 200g (7oz) filet mignon to the beefier 700g (24oz) Porterhouse. **$$**

French

French cuisine is characterised by its universal acclaim, and though much of it has become centralised on Paris, each region of France has developed its own culinary specialities. Provençal cuisine favours olive oil and herbs; while Alsatian is influenced by Germanic traditions. Both are represented.

La Berengerie
Montague and Clanton roads
Tel: 250 539 5392
Small and genteel French restaurant.

Bistro Pastis
2153 West 4th Avenue
Tel: 604 731 5020
In a lively district, this French bistro is in the heart of Kitsilano. Quality traditional fare, such as coq au vin or steak tartare and frites, are prepared with a light touch. **$$$**

Café de Paris Bistro
751 Denman Street
Tel: 604 687 1418
Orthodox Gallic cooking in this traditional

French bistro imitates the offerings you might find in the heart of Paris – steak au poivre, cassoulet and bouillabaisse. **$$$**

Le Crocodile
909 Burrard Street, entrance on Smithe
Tel: 604 669 4298
Monet's Giverny garden sets the tone for this refined setting for French-Alsatian food with solidly flavoured dishes. Dine among jet setters and visiting celebrities. **$$$**

Le Gavroche
1616 Alberni Street
Tel: 604 685 3924
Cosy, classy restaurant, which for more than 20 years has been serving up excellent dishes such as rack of lamb and veal. **$$$**

Southeast Asian

Vancouver has an ever growing love affair with southeast Asian cuisines, including Malaysian, Indonesian, Vietnamese and Thai. Soups and noodles, curries and satays (grilled meat with peanut sauce) influence these dishes. Thai food incorporates sweet, sour, salty and sometimes fiery hot (you can often choose how hot you want it to be) flavours. Asian food is eaten with a spoon, not chopsticks.

Banana Leaf on Broadway
Banana Leaf on Denman
820 West Broadway Tel: 604 731 6333
1096 Denman Street. Tel: 604 683 3333
Simple tropical accents – bamboo plants and large fans – adorn these two award-winning Malaysian restaurants, which serve delicious authentic food: mild, hot or super-spicy dishes. **$$**

Monsoon Restaurant
2526 Main Street and Broadway
Tel: 604 879 4001
An East-meets-West brasserie with loads of atmosphere, this restaurant is rather small and always busy – buoyed on by its proven Asian-Thai fusion menu and good drinks. **$$**

Montri's Thai Restaurant
3629 West Broadway
Tel: 604 738 9888
With Western rather than Thai decor, this establishment is fresh and friendly, and serves well prepared classics like tom yum goong (prawn and lemon grass soup). **$$**

Phnom Penh
244 East Georgia Street
Tel: 604 682 5777
This Vietnamese/Cambodian restaurant in the heart of Chinatown may look uninviting, but inside it's peaceful and friendly. Try lemongrass chicken, exemplary hot and sour soups or garlic-pepper seafood. **$$**

Salathai Restaurant
3364 Cambie Street
Tel: 604 875 6999
Three talented chefs from five-star hotels in Bangkok and Pattaya create dishes fit for the Thai royal family (who eat here during their visits to Vancouver), and it's won accolades from discerning diners. **$$$**

Vegetarian

Vancouver is Canada's premier vegetarian-friendly city and this is a small selection of the places, some inspired by the Buddist movement, that serve meat-free and vegan food.

Bo Kong
3068 Main Street
Tel: 604 876 1328
A Buddhist Chinese restaurant with a mostly vegan menu of items such as hot and sour thick soup, spring rolls and deep fried soya

Foundation Lounge
2301 Main Street
Tel: 604 708 0881
Funky open-concept space with a fabulous view and unique-but-affordable items such as black bean and banana. **$**

Above: Vancouver's oldest vegetarian haven

Greens and Gourmet
2582 West Broadway
Tel: 604 737 7373
Greenery-filled rooms and New-Age music create a pleasant atmosphere for the salad bar and hot buffet. Specialities: moussaka and honey-miso tofu. Natural desserts and pastries are mostly wheat- and dairy-free. **$$**

Planet Veg
1941 Cornwall Street
Tel: 604 734 1001
Most popular veggie spot in the city, serving meat-free fast food. The tasty Garden Burger is served with yam and apple chutney.

The Naam
2724 West 4th Avenue
Tel: 604 738 7151
Vancouver's oldest vegetarian restaurant is funky, cosy and still generating queues for their huge house salads and yummy sesame fries with miso gravy. Open 24 hours. **$**

Yogi's Vegetarian Indian Cuisine
1408 Commercial Drive
Tel: 604 251 9644
Permanently on 'best vegetarian' lists, the focus here is on food not furniture. Smells, colours and texture combine for an authentic Punjabi vegetarian experience. **$**

Latin American
From Peru, the potato; from Argentina, cattle and sheep; southern continental waters provide tuna and Chile gives us the word for chilli. Traditional Latin cooking from Spain and Portugal sometimes involves outdoor fires and one custom well adapted to the city lifestyle is an afternoon snack, tapas.

Havana
1212 Commercial Drive
Tel: 604 253 9119
The food has an Afro-Latin flavour at this funky, cool place on the East Side. **$**

Baru Latino
2535 Alma Street
Tel: 604 222 9171
Voted 'Best of the Americas', this authentic Colombian tapas spot is a place where upbeat music matches lively specialities. **$**

La Bodega
1277 Howe Street
Tel: 604 684 8815
Since 1971 this popular downtown tapateria has served Spanish favourites such as garlic prawns, *patatas bravas* and sangria. **$$**

Latin Quarter
1305 Commercial Drive
Tel: 604 251 1144
A local hole-in-the-wall hangout where life revolves around the kitchen, bar and a small stage. Classic Iberian tapas. **$$**

Rinconcito Salvadorean Restaurant
2062 Commercial Drive
Tel: 604 879 2600
Central American fare in a tropical setting presents seaks, tacos and *camarone ranchero* (prawns in spicy tomato sauce), a good introduction to Salvadorean cooking. **$**

Just Desserts
In spite of a preoccupation with healthy living, Vancouverites are not averse to a delicious sweet ending to their meal. Ice cream, cake or pastry, or a more sumptuous concoctions are on offer at these Vancouver establishments devoted to sugar highs.

Death By Chocolate
1001 Denman Street
Tel: 604 899 2462
A photo album of 30 decadent desserts with seductive names: Between the Sheets, Crumble In My Arms, or A Multitude of Sins. **$$**

Sweet Revenge Patisserie
4160 Main Street
Tel: 604 879 7933
This pastry shop serves traditional European delights – crème brûlée, white chocolate cheesecake, ganache-covered torte cake, speciality teas and coffees and dessert wines. **$** (cash only)

True Confections
866 Denman Street
Tel: 604 682 1292
Around 60 desserts are on offer here, all mouthwatering originals based on old family recipes. The lemon cheesecake is as close to heaven as you can get. **$$**

NIGHTLIFE

More than 150,000 people live in the urban core and these are the people who set the tone of the city. Vancouver has a busy and generally safe night-time street scene. People are out dancing, dining or just strolling along the avenues as evening falls. They feed a counter-culture theatre scene and staff the summer festivals. Compared to many cities however, nightlife past midnight is pretty tame here. Some say it's because Vancouverites are so health conscious, preferring early morning jogs to dawn-busting raves. Culture tends to be on a small scale, driven by coteries of talented artists on tight budgets, but what they produce is rich and varied. There's a degree of federal support, but the vibrant arts community is largely ignored by local businesses; until sponsorship evolves, city venues, the symphony, opera, theatre and rising artists will remain trapped.

Granville Street, between Robson and Drake, is the entertainment district and the Commodore, Orpheum, Vogue, Paradise, Granville, Caprice and Capitol theatres are the legacy of the late 1920s–40s heyday of 'Theatre Row'. Advance tickets for all major events are available through TicketMaster, tel: 604 280 3311. Purchase immediate entertainment tickets at a discount from Tickets Tonight, tel: 604 684 ARTS (684 2787). The most useful guide for just about everything in Vancouver is the free weekly, *Georgia Strait*.

Professional Sports
General Motors Place
Beneath the Georgia Street Viaduct
Tel: 604 899 7400 for hockey tickets

Host to the National Hockey League's (NHL) Vancouver Canucks; the most advanced venue of its kind in North America.

BC Place Stadium
777 Pacific Boulevard
Tel: 604 930 5466
Home to the Canadian Football League's (CFL) BC Lions from June to late October; also hosts major conventions, trade shows and monster truck shows.

Theatre

In addition to the places listed below, there are two outdoor theatrical venues in summer. **Bard on the Beach** (Vanier Park, tel: 604 739 0559) features Shakespeare plays in a circus tent; the **Theatre under the Stars** (Malkin Bowl, Stanley Park, tel: 604 687 0174) stages musicals under canvas. Performances at both start at 8.30pm.

Vancouver Playhouse
630 Hamilton, near Georgia Street
Tel: 604 873 3311
This is Vancouver's main stage for both traditional and contemporary theatre.

Arts Club Theatre
1585 Johnston Street, Granville Island
Tel: 604 687 1644
Two professional companies offer a range of plays from comedies to human drama.

Stanley Theatre
2780 Granville Street
Tel: 604 687 1644
Quaint, 1920s art-deco style theatre hosting vibrant, small, innovative productions.

Centre in Vancouver for the Performing Arts
777 Homer Street
Tel: 604 602 0616
Large theatre with great sightlines and acoustics for big-name musical productions.

Vogue Theatre
918 Granville Street
Tel: 604 280 4444
A small theatre, dance and music venue within a heritage building; modern works.

Classical Music and Opera

Orpheum
601 Smithe Street
Tel: 604 688 5000
Fine heritage theatre with first-class acoustics. Home of the Vancouver Symphony.

Queen Elizabeth Theatre
630 Hamilton near Georgia
Tel: 604 683 0222
The Vancouver Opera performs four major works a year here.

Comedy Clubs

Gastown Comedy Store
19 Water Street
Tel: 604 682 1727
Comedy acts, and also interactive murder mysteries and magic; reservations advised.

Yuk Yuks Comedy Club
750 Pacific Boulevard South
Tel: 604 687 5233
Stand-up and improvisational comedy by touring professionals; reservations advised.

Jazz Clubs

Cover charges vary. The Jazz Hotline (tel: 604 872 5200) lists the latest events.

Cellar Jazz
3611 West Broadway (downstairs)
Tel: 604 738 1959
Laid back jazz with a bit of funk, soul and R&B; cover charge.

Hot Jazz
2120 Main Street
Tel: 604 873 4131
A hot spot for live big-band and swing; cover.

Dance Clubs

Dance Centre hotline, tel: 604 606 6400.

Au Bar
674 Seymour Street
Tel: 604 648 2227
Hot and usually packed, this is a place to see and be seen, with nightly top 40 DJ music.

Babalu
654 Nelson, at Granville
Tel: 604 605 4343
A Cuban-style lounge with big band sounds, this is a lively and often crowded venue.

Commodore Ballroom
868 Granville Street
Tel: 739 4550
Built in 1929; has great sound and a massive sprung dance floor.

Live Music

Purple Onion Cabaret
15 Water Street
Tel: 604 602 9442
DJ playing 1980s and 90s hip-hop one side and live jazz/blues on the other.

Richards on Richards
1036 Richards, at Nelson
Tel: 604 687 6794
On weekends it's a live music dance club for over 30s. Dress code.

Lively Pubs and Bars

Bar None
1222 Hamilton in Yaletown
Tel: 604 689 7000
Beautiful people come for the live bands, pool table and a good house band Mon and Tues.

Fairview Pub
898 West Broadway
Tel: 604 872 1262
Jazz Thurs night, rhythm and blues the rest of the week; weekends for dancing.

Skybar
670 Smithe Street
Tel: 604 697 9199
Partying on three levels, with two bars and a retractable roof. Open Wed–Sat. A hot spot.

Left: hanging out on Granville Street

CALENDAR OF EVENTS

Vancouver celebrates with lively festivals throughout the year, but summer is particularly active. Book well in advance if there is a specific event you wish to attend. the Greater Vancouver Visitors and Convention Bureau have details on their website (www.tourismvancouver.com) or you can call for information (tel: 604 683 2000).

JANUARY / FEBRUARY

January 1. **The Polar Bear Swim Club** ushers in the New Year in the icy waters of English Bay; tel: 604 665 3418 to participate.

Early January. The **Canadian Free Skiing Championship** in Whistler. Tel: 604 932 3434.

Late January. **Burns' Night celebration** in Harrison Hot Springs. With Scottish cultural events. Tel: 604 796 2574 for hotel reservations.

February. The venerable **BC Home and Garden Show** is held in BC Place Stadium for an extended period; a massive trade show featuring celebrity guests. Tel: 604 433 5121.

Late February. A fortnight of **Chinese New Year celebrations** includes fireworks, feasts and parades. Dates vary according to the Chinese calendar. Tel: 604 683 2000.

The nine-day **International Mountain Film Festival** in North Vancouver presents film events about mountain culture and sport. Tel: 604 990 1505.

MARCH / APRIL

Mid-March. Regional and international wine tastings are part of the week-long **Vancouver Playhouse International Wine Festival**. Tel: 604 874 3311.

The award-winning week-long **CelticFest** includes performance, art and a **St Patrick's Day Parade**. Tel: 604 683 8331.

The **Artists in our Midst** event features more than 70 Vancouver artists who invite visitors into their homes, studios and galleries every weekend in April. Admission is free. Tel: 604 224 3238.

Early-April. The week-long **TELUS World Ski and Snowboard Festival** at Whistler resort includes races, demonstrations, concerts, a dog parade, late-night fun and fireworks. Tel: 604 932 5528.

Mid-April. The city's **Sikh community celebrates Baisakhi**, birth of the Khalsa, with parades that begin or end at the Ross Street temple, Marine Drive. Tel: 604 324 2010.

The **Vancouver Sun Run** is one of Canada's largest 10-km (6-mile) races; live bands spur participants on to the party at the end of the race. Tel: 604 689 9441.

For some of the best whale watching try the month-long **Pacific Rim Whale Festival** on Vancouver Island, which celebrates the northward migration of some 20,000 gray whales. Tel: 250 726 4641 (Ucluelet Chamber of Commerce); Tel: 250 725 3414 (Tofino Chamber of Commerce).

MAY

Mid-May. The eight-day **Vancouver International Children's Festival** at Vanier Park features top international acts and storytellers in big-top tents. Tel: 604 708 5655.

Mid-May–Sept. The **Artcraft Summer Sale** is the umbrella name for the Gulf Islands' gathering of artworks held in Mahon Hall at Ganges on Salt Spring Island Wed–Sat. The **Salt Spring Island Annual Studio Tour** is part of the event; dozens of artisans invite visitors into their studios. Participants include a wood-fired bakery and a cheese-making company. Tel: 250 537 5252 or 250 537 4223.

20 May. The four-day **Cloverdale Rodeo and Exhibition** in Surrey features top bronco- and bull-riders, steer-wrestlers and calf-ropers. Tel: 604 576 9461.

The cheerful **Island Farms Victoria Day Parade** in downtown Victoria, along Douglas Street, features clowns and marching bands. Held on the May holiday weekend (around 24 May) to commemorate Queen Victoria's birthday. Tel: 250 382 3111.

JUNE / JULY

Early June. The four-day **VanDusen Flower and Garden Show** is held in a spectacular outdoor setting with display gardens by more than 250 exhibitors. Tel: 604 878 6700.

Mid-June. At False Creek about 100 local and international teams compete in the **Canadian International Dragon Boat Festival**. Tel: 604 688 2382.

Late June. Two weeks of jazz, blues and

fusion music feature in the massive (Vancouver) **International Jazz Festival**. Tel: 604 872 5200.

JazzFest International in Victoria features hundreds of musicians. Tel: 250 388 4423.

Vancouver Greek Day has bouzouki dancing and Greek food in Kitsilano. Tel: 604 683 2000.

1 July. **Canada Day** is celebrated with parties and fireworks. Tel: 604 683 2000.

Mid-July. The two-day **Vancouver Folk Music Festival** at Jericho Beach park features international performers and craft booths. Tel: 604 602 9798.

Mid-July. Coast Salish teams take part in the informal **Squamish Nation War Canoe Races**, at Ambleside Beach. Tel: 604 980 4553.

Late July. The **Tour de Gastown** competitive bicycle race is always a Vancouver tour de force. Tel: 604 836 9993.

In Victoria, the three-day **Walking with Our Ancestors Cultural Celebration** at the Victoria Native Friendship Centre is the nation's largest exhibition of First Nation's storytellers, drummers, designers and dance traditions. Tel: 250 384 3211.

End July. **Powell Street Festival** in Oppenheimer Park is a celebration of Japanese culture and heritage, with martial arts, sumo, taiko and kabuki theatre. Tel: 604 739 9388.

Late July/early August. The nightskies light up with the **Celebration of Light**'s free fireworks shows around English Bay. Tel: 604 682 6839 for dates and information.

AUGUST

Early August. A colourful parade is part of the **Gay Pride Festival**. Tel: 604 683 2000.

Early August. **Festival Vancouver** assembles classical, jazz and world musicians from various countries to present concerts at venues throughout British Columbia. Tel: 604 688 1152.

The week-long **Crankworx Free Ride Mountain Bike Festival** at Whistler showcases the world's best mountain bikers zipping down mountains and performing death-defying stunts. Tel: 604 932 5528.

Late August–Labour Day. The **Fair at the PNE** (Pacific National Exhibition) at Hastings Park is one of North America's largest agri-fairs, with an ambitious variety of concerts, dog shows, pig races, demonstrations, and an amusement park. Tel: 604 253 2311.

SEPTEMBER / OCTOBER

Mid- to late September. The zany **Vancouver Fringe Festival** has up to 100 small stage alternative events. Tel: 604 257 0350.

Early October. The **International Comedy Festival** on Granville Island has comedians, skit troupes and buskers. Tel: 604 685 0260.

Late September/early October. The **Mid-Autumn Moon Festival** is a romantic Chinese cultural event with colourful lanterns, myth telling, tea and mooncakes at Dr Sun Yat-Sen Classical Garden. Tel: 604 662 3207.

Mid-October. The two-day Oktoberfest in Whistler, has mugs of beer, music and thigh-slapping folk dancers. Tel: 604 932 5528.

NOVEMBER / DECEMBER

Early November. The **Circle Craft Christmas Market** is an enormous gathering showcasing artisan crafts. Tel: 604 801 5220.

Early December. The **North American Native Arts & Crafts Festival** at the Aboriginal Friendship Centre also has traditional dance and food. Tel: 604 253 1020.

December. The nightly **Christmas Carol Ship Parade** sees more than 80 boat owners light up their vessels and take (paying) guests on moonlight cruises. Tel: 604 878 8999.

Right: celebrating Chinese New Year

Practical Information

GETTING THERE

By Air

Vancouver International Airport is 16km (10 miles) from the downtown area, servicing regional (south terminal) and worldwide destinations, particularly the Pacific Rim. An airport levy on departure varies from $5–$15 depending on destination. Taxis to downtown are currently around $35. A less costly airport express bus leaves for major hotels every 30 minutes. Travellers with luggage should try to avoid public transport.

By Rail

Via Rail (www.viarail.ca) has a trans-continental service with stops including Jasper and Toronto departs Vancouver three times weekly, tel: 1 888 842 7245 or 514 989 2626; from UK tel: 0845 644 3553; from Australia tel: 61 2 9319 6624. Amtrak has reintroduced passenger service from Seattle to Vancouver, tel: 1 800 872 7245 for more details. BC Rail goes to Prince George and the interior of British Columbia, tel: 604 984 5246.

By Road

From the US/Seattle take Interstate 5 north through the 24-hour Canadian customs at Peace Arch/Blaine (up to an hour's daytime wait) and follow Highway 99 north into Vancouver. Crossing the Granville Bridge take Seymour north into downtown. From Eastern BC and Canada, Trans-Canada Highway 1 and 1A connect to Vancouver. For BC road conditions tel: 1 900 451 4997.

By Sea

BC Ferries Corporation (www.bcferries.com) has one of the world's largest ferry fleets, with sailings at least every two hours, more in summer. For ferries to Vancouver Island/Nanaimo and the Sunshine Coast take Highway 1A-99 north to the Horseshoe Bay terminal (crowded on summer weekends).

For Victoria, South Vancouver Island and the Gulf Islands, take 1A south to Highway 17 and the Tsawwassen ferry terminal. For 24-hour ferry information anywhere in British Columbia, tel: 1 888 223 3779, from outside BC, tel: 250 386 3431. By bus via BC Ferries go via Pacific Coach Lines (www.pacificcoach.com), tel: 1 800 661 1725 or 604 662 7575.

TRAVEL ESSENTIALS

Visitor Information

Accommodation and Travel Information for BC SuperNatural British Columbia information and reservations service, nicknamed 'Hello BC!', will provide brochures and information as well as making hotel bookings (www.hellobc.com; tel: 1 800 435 5622 in North America; 604 435 5622 from Vancouver; tel: 250 387 1642 from overseas.

BC Parks To find the location of provincially operated parks and campgrounds in British Columbia (www.govbc.ca/bcparks). Each of the hundreds of parks has its own office phone number. British Columbia is also home to seven federally administered National Parks.

BC Coalition of People with Disabilities, 204–456 West Broadway, Vancouver V5Y IR3, tel: 604 875 0188.

Vancouver Travel Infocentre Multilingual

Left: a harbour view from Canada Place
Right: Canadian customs sign

representatives provide accommodation bookings, car rentals, maps and brochures (tel: 604 683 2000; www.tourismvancouver.com). Drop into Tourism Vancouver at the Waterfront Centre (Plaza level, 200 Burrard Street at Cordova; Mon–Sat 9am–5pm, Sun noon–5pm.) The organisation also runs a summer-only kiosk in the Pacific Centre Mall at Robson and Hornby.

Victoria Travel Infocentre For travel bookings and information, drop into 812 Wharf Street, Victoria (tel: 250 953 2033, 1 800 663 3883 [toll free in Canada]; www.tourismvictoria.com).

Whistler Travel Infocentre Designated as the site of the 2010 Winter Olympics, the Whistler centre provides services ranging from renting condominiums and hotels to previewing ski and outdoor experiences. Drop into Tourism Whistler, 4010 Whistler Way, Whistler (tel: 604 664 5625 or toll free in Canada and the US, 1 800 WHISTLER; fax: 604 932 7231; www.mywhistler.com).

GETTING ACQUAINTED

Geography

Vancouver has a coastal rainforest climate. It is surrounded on three sides by water, Burrard Inlet to the north, the Fraser River to the south and the Strait of Georgia between the city and Vancouver Island. The coast mountains rise 3,000m (9,840ft) to the east. Population growth into the mountains is limited by the need to protect the city's drinking water sources, so most urban growth is in the communities of the Fraser River delta to the south and east.

The heart of Vancouver is a peninsula comprising the downtown, West End and Stanley Park areas. False Creek, a small saltwater inlet, separates downtown from its southern neighbourhoods of Fairview, Kitsilano, West Point Grey and others. To the north, across Burrard Inlet at the base of the Coast Range, are the residential communities of West Vancouver and North Vancouver.

Government

Vancouver City Council consists of the mayor and nine city councillors, elected every three years. Victoria is the seat of the provincial legislature, and Vancouver is divided into 10 provincial electoral districts. Representatives are elected from the Liberal and New Democratic parties. Vancouver also elects five members to the Federal Government of Canada.

Economy

Forestry, tourism, mining and international trade are key industries, making British Columbia the most volatile economy in Canada. Vancouver is an emergent international financial centre and the largest port in North America in terms of import and export tonnage. Vancouver is a major film and TV production centre, variously nicknamed 'Hollywood North' and 'Brollywood' (because it rains more here than California).

Population

Migration from the provinces and immigration from the Pacific Rim countries make Vancouver's 16 percent annual growth rate the second fastest in Canada and the fourth fastest in North America (40,000 people per year). The population of Vancouver city is 550,000, with 2.1 million in the metropolitan area (2002 census). Of this latter figure about 365,000 are of English descent and there are 61 recognized immigrant communities within the city limits. At 200,000 the Asian community is the largest.

Etiquette

Vancouverites are polite and friendly with just a touch of reserve. They are used to

Left: feeding the ducks in Stanley Park

Weather

Warm Pacific currents bathe Vancouver in mild weather throughout the year, and Vancouver Island shelters the city from Pacific storms. Snow seldom falls, but persistent cloud cover with frequent light rain is the rule between November and May. Summer high temperatures range between 17–25°C (67–80°F), winter temperatures between 5–11°C (41–52°F). For British Columbia weather reports, tel: 604 664 9010.

Clothing

Casual to casual-dressy is the rule. On summer nights a light sweater or a windbreaker will keep you comfortable. Bring an umbrella and SPF15 or higher sunscreen too, as the weather is very changeable. In winter bring raingear and waterproof footwear.

Electricity

Canada uses 120 volts AC.

Time Differences

The city of Vancouver is on Pacific Standard Time, GMT/UTC minus 8 hours, with Daylight Saving Time in effect between early April and late October.

MONEY MATTERS

Currency

Canadian money is in dollars and cents. Dollar bills come in denominations of five, 10 and 20. The one-dollar coin is known as the 'looney', the two-dollar coin the 'twoney'. The value of the Canadian dollar fluctuates in relation to its US counterpart and all world currencies. All prices quoted in this book are in Canadian dollars.

Credit Cards and Cheques

Major credit cards and travellers cheques are accepted virtually everywhere. Exchange rates vary widely. Check with foreign exchange offices, which you'll find near Georgia and Burrard, or one of the 25 foreign banks in the city.

Cash Machines (ATMs)

These are found in bank foyers and large stores. Most international cards are accepted. Many have 24-hour, card-only secure access.

sharing their city and will go to unusual lengths to help a visitor. When referring to indigenous peoples, use the term First Nations and Inuit – never Indian and Eskimo.

When to Visit

Vancouver belongs to travellers during the warm, sometimes wet summer (June–Sept). Locals take their vacations in August, and September, when it is still warm, is the most popular month for tourists. The best winter months are February, the height of the ski season, and March, famous for spring-skiing.

Visas and Passports

There are no visa requirements for visitors from Australia, Japan, the UK and the US, but passports are necessary. Please note that a driving licence does *not* constitute sufficient identification. European travellers should verify visa requirements with Canadian consulates in their home country as some restrictions may apply.

Customs

There are no currency restrictions. Travellers may take advantage of duty-free shopping. Contact the customs office for details of duty requirements (tel: 1 800 461 9999 or tel: 204 983 3500 from outside Canada).

Top: a view over Lions Gate Bridge

Tipping
Tips are not included in your bills or taxi fares; 15–20 percent is the norm.

Taxes
A 7 percent provincial sales tax applies to purchases except groceries and books. An additional Federal Goods and Services Tax (GST) of 7 percent is added to all purchases except groceries. Foreign visitors may apply for tax refunds on accommodation, and consumer goods for export. Keep receipts and ask for rebate forms at your hotel.

GETTING AROUND

On Foot
Some 15km (9 miles) of walking and biking trails provide breathtaking views from numerous vantage points along the waterfront from Stanley Park around False Creek to Kitsilano. If you walk across any of the bridges stay close to the railings, as cyclists speed along the inside of the walkway.

Taxis
You will find taxis at hotels and taxi-stands throughout the city. Rates start at $2.40 and accrue at $1.70 per kilometre, tax included. Cabs are clean and comfortable.

Bus and SkyTrain
Bus routes and the SkyTrain are commuter-oriented. Faresaver block tickets are sold in stores displaying red and blue Fare-Dealer signs. Transfers are valid for return bus trips within 90 minutes, and also valid for the SeaBus and SkyTrain. Contact Translink, tel: 604 953 3333; www.translink.bc.ca.

Passenger Ferries and SeaBus
The SeaBus leaves the old CPR station at Cordova (due north from Robson Square) for North Vancouver's Lonsdale Quay every 15 minutes until midnight. The Granville Island ferries make quick jaunts across False Creek from the foot of Thurlow Street downtown.

By Car
Vancouver does not have freeways entering the central business district and traffic jams are a major problem. However, driving is safe and sedate. Speed limits are measured in metric and they are strictly enforced by photo radar. Parking penalties are common.

HOURS AND HOLIDAYS

Business Hours
Shops are open 7 days a week, although a few are closed on Monday. Most open at 10am, some later at weekends. Closing times vary, but downtown stores open late on weekdays in summer, closing at 6pm Sat–Sun.

Market Days
Granville Island Market Fresh food, crafts and flowers (daily 9am–6pm).
Lonsdale Quay North Vancouver market with retailers, crafts and food (daily 9.30am–6.30pm, Fri until 9pm).

Public Holidays

New Year	1 January
Good Friday	date varies
Victoria Day	3rd Monday in May
Canada Day	1 July
BC Day	1st Monday in August
Labour Day	1st Monday in Sept

Thanksgiving	2nd Monday in October
Remembrance Day	11 November
Christmas Day	25 December
Boxing Day	26 December

ACCOMMODATION

There is a choice of landmark hotels, lodges and comfy B&Bs throughout Vancouver, Victoria and Whistler. Rates are listed in Canadian dollars and are based on a nightly double-occupancy stay.

$ = under $85
$$ = $85–$160
$$$ = more than $160

Blue Horizon
1225 Robson at Butte
Tel: 604 688 1411 (1 800 633 1333 toll free in Canada); wwwbluehorizonhotel.com
The Blue Horizon's renovated rooms are huge, with balconies and most have excellent views. The 214-room hotel is located between Stanley Park and Robson Square.
$$–$$$

Fairmont Hotel Vancouver
900 West Georgia Street
Tel: 604 684 3131 (1 800 441 1414 toll free in Canada; 0800 389 4000 from overseas) www.fairmont.com
With its chateau-style copper roof, this is an original Canadian Pacific Hotel, with 556 rooms and high standards of service. Amenities include a spa, pool and gym. **$$$**

Fairmont Waterfront
900 Canada Place Way, at the foot of Howe
Tel: 604 691 1991 (1 800 441 1414 toll free in Canada); www.fairmont.com/waterfront
Good local art decorates this glass tower, a luxury hotel with a grand airy entrance and generous rooms and suites. Service and amenities are excellent. Just above Burrard Inlet, with harbour views from 75 percent of the 489 rooms. **$$$**

Four Seasons Hotel
791 West Georgia at Howe
Tel: 604 689 9333 (1 800 332 3442 toll free from US); www.fourseasons.com/vancouver
The ultimate in luxury, sited above a 200-

store shopping mall. The 385-room hotel has impeccable standards and its Chartwell restaurant is undoubtedly one of the city's best. **$$$**

Four Seasons Resort Whistler
4591 Blackcomb Way, Whistler
Tel: 604 935 3400
www.fourseasons.com/whistler
Luxury in the mountains, this 273-room hotel is walking distance from the ski lift in the Upper Village. All rooms and suites have a fireplace and balcony. **$$$**

Greenbriar
1393 Robson Street
Tel: 604 683 4558 (1 800 355 5888 toll free in Canada); www.greenbriarhotel.com
The Greenbriar is well-known for its good value, one-bedroom and family suites, and some have good views too. It's conveniently located near Stanley Park and English Bay.
$$

Pan Pacific
300–999 Canada Place
Tel: 662 8111 (1 800-663 1515 toll free in Canada; 1 800 937 1515 from USA; www.panpacific.com
A fabulous property on Canada Place Pier, with top ratings for both the hotel accommodation and the Five Sails restaurant. **$$$**

Left: an Aquabus at Granville Island
Top: the landmark Hotel Vancouver

Sutton Place
845 Burrard Street
Tel: 604 682 5511 (1 800 961 7555, toll free
in Canada); www.suttonplace.com
Elegant marble and fresh flowers abound in
this 397-room luxury hotel. The lounge is
a popular hangout with the film and corpo-
rate after-work crowd. $$$

Sylvia Hotel
1154 Gilford at Beach Avenue
Tel: 604 681 9321; www.sylviahotel.com
This is an ivy covered, European-style
heritage hotel on English Bay, with lively
Denman Street and Stanley Park near by.
One of the best locations in the city, and even
though it isn't fancy and service isn't top
notch, the 119-room Sylvia is a legend. $$

Inns, Lodges and B&Bs

Edelweiss Pension
7162 Nancy Greene Way, Whistler
Tel: 604 932 3641;
A lovely European-influenced pension
owned by retired French Olympic ski coach
Jacques Morel. With an old-world intimacy
prevalent in the design covenants through-
out the valley. $$

English Bay Inn
1968 Comox at Chilco
Tel: 604 683 8002 (1 866 683 8002 toll free
in Canada); www.englishbayinn.com
Romantic, antique, this classic Tudor house
is located just a block from Stanley Park
and English Bay. It has five guest rooms,
each with private bathroom and phone. No
smoking. $$$

Johnson Heritage House B&B
2278 West 34th Avenue
Tel: 604 266 4175
Located in the Kerrisdale neighbourhood,
this bed-and-breakfast home is just a short
walk from local restaurants. No smoking;
no credit cards. $$

Penny Farthing Inn
2855 West 6th Avenue
Tel: 604 739 9002
www.pennyfarthinginn.com
Restored heritage house with antiques, in a
quiet street 1.5km (1 mile) from downtown.

Some rooms have mountain views and there
are cafés near by. No smoking. $$

Kenya Court Oceanfront Guesthouse
2230 Cornwall in Kitsilano
Tel: 604 738 7085
A 1920s guesthouse across from Kitsilano
Beach, with four large one- and two-
bedroom suites and a rooftop solarium where
a complimentary breakfast is served. No
smoking; no credit cards. The guest house
charges per person and not by room like most
other places. $$

HOSTEL
Hostelling International Vancouver
Jericho Beach
1515 Discovery, near 4th Avenue
Tel: 604 224 3208; www.hihostels.ca
A 285-bed dormitory with a restaurant and
kitchens for self-catering, plus mountain bike
rental. The hostel is in a wonderful setting,
but it is more than 30 minutes from down-
town Vancouver, on one of the worst public
transit routes. $

HEALTH AND
EMERGENCIES

Pharmacies
There are numerous pharmacies. Shoppers
Drug Mart at Davie and Thurlow (tel: 604
685 6445) is open 24 hours.

Medical and Dental Services
Visitors in need of a doctor or dentist on
weekdays may attend drop-in clinics at the
Medicentre (tel: 604 683 8138) or Denta-
centre (tel: 604 669 6700), both in the Bental
Centre at Burrard and Dunsmuir. At other
times Vancouver General Hospital emer-
gency department is the quickest way to get
medical attention. Be sure to invest in
holiday medical insurance to cover costs.

Crime
Petty theft and pan-handling have become
noticeable problems in Vancouver and
Victoria. Theft from parked cars is a prob-
lem everywhere; don't leave items visible in
an unattended vehicle. Break-ins are com-
mon to rental vehicles parked in apparently
secure hotel underground garages. Women

Right: cycling in Stanley Park

are advised to guard their bags while dining or sightseeing. Night-time walking in most areas downtown is generally safe and popular, though street drugs and vendors are not uncommon. If your personal comfort level feels challenged, it's best to avoid drug-infested areas, notably in East Vancouver.

In an emergency dial **911** from any telephone for police, fire or ambulance.

COMMUNICATIONS AND NEWS

Post
Canada post offices are found throughout the city, but people often use the mini-outlets located in convenience stores and pharmacies. Look for the Canada Post signs on buildings and in store windows. Hours vary, and services are often available at weekends.

Telephone
The country code for Canada is 1. Area codes are: **604** for Vancouver, Fraser Valley and Whistler and **250** elsewhere. Dial 0 for operator assistance and 411 for information.

Media
The afternoon *Vancouver Sun* and the morning *Province* are the local daily newspapers. There are 12 community papers. The *Georgia Straight*, published each Thursday, is the best free compendium of issues and events. *Vancouver* magazine is a good city monthly. There are numerous TV channels and more than 20 radio stations, many in foreign languages The Canadian Broadcasting Company (CBC; on 93.1FM/690AM) is one of the finest ways to get to know Canada. Best in-town newsstand for out-of-town news: Mayfair News, 1535 West Broadway, off Granville, tel: 604 738 8951. In the hotel and business district Sophia Books at 492 West Hastings Street, tel: 604 684 0484, specialises in foreign-language books and periodicals.

SPORTS/OUTDOOR RECREATION

To many Vancouverites being outdoors is the most important thing in their lives. The mountains, beaches, rivers, lakes and ocean have created limitless possibilities for recreation. Here are just a few ideas.

Biking: Stanley Park anchors the downtown core with miles of trails into the heart of the park (see Day 2 Itinerary, page 26). The seawall links up with the 15-km (9½-mile) Vancouver Seaside Bicycle Route at the south end of the park.

Salmon fishing: Sewell's Marina (tel: 604 921 3474) at Horseshoe Bay supplies everything from rod and bait to boats.

Golf: Vancouver Parks and Recreation operates three full-length municipal courses and three pitch and putt courses. The most challenging full-length course is McCleery Golf Course, tel: 604 257 8191. Other notable city courses open to the public are the University Golf Club at UBC, tel: 604 224 1818; Mayfair Lakes in Richmond, tel: 604 276 0505; Gleneagles in West Vancouver, tel: 604 921 7353.

Hiking: For the casual and avid hiker Mount Seymour Provincial Park (tel: 604 986 2261) provides alpine meadows and views of the Coast Range and Georgia Strait.

Hot Air Ballooning: balloon rides over the farmlands of the Fraser Valley with Fantasy Balloon Charters, tel: 604 530 1974.

River Rafting: Some of the most exciting big-water rapids in North America are on the Fraser and Thompson rivers. Contact Hyak Wilderness Adventures, tel: 604 734 8622 or Fraser River Rafting, tel: 1 800 363 7238.

Sea Kayaking: Ecomarine (tel: 604 689 7575) operates two rental outlets on Granville Island and Jericho Beach, suitable for novices and experienced paddlers.

Tennis: The city Board of Parks and Recreation operates 180 courts (no charge) throughout the city. Six courts in Stanley Park can be reserved (tel: 604 257 8400).

Windsurfing: Jericho Sailing 'MacSailing' Centre (tel: 604 224 4177) is the best for this sport. Try also Windsure Windsurfing (tel: 604 224 0615) for rentals and lessons.

Spectator Sports

Baseball: The Oakland Athletic's Single A affiliate (farm team), the Vancouver Canadians, play ball throughout the summer at Nat Bailey Stadium (4601 Ontario Street, tel:604 872-5232), a classic minor-league field with a scenic backdrop.

Hockey: The Vancouver Canucks, of the National Hockey League (NHL) play the world's fastest game at General Motors (GM) Place Oct–May. Tickets available (as long as the hockey lock-out and strike is resolved) from Ticketmaster, tel: 604 280 4400. For hockey with heart (and cheaper tickets) check out the popular Vancouver Giants, a hard-hitting farm team grooming young players for the big leagues. Tel: 604 280 4400 for tickets.

Football: The championship winning BC Lions play in the Canadian Football League (CFL), a US-style football game but with three downs and slightly different field dimensions and markings. For information contact Ticketmaster, tel: 604 280 4400.

Horse Racing: Harness horseracing takes place at Fraser Downs Raceway in Surrey. For race times, tel: 604 576 9141.

USEFUL INFORMATION

Travellers with Disabilities
People with physical disabilities will find that Vancouver is a wheelchair-friendly city, and wheelchair users are active. The stop lights 'chirp' for the sight impaired at some crossings.

Children
With so many people living downtown, well-mannered drivers and good natured people, it's a kids' city. Itineraries of particular interest to kids include: Itinerary 2, with Stanley Park's wading pools, water parks, miniature train and aquarium; Itinerary 3, with Granville Island and its water park, lawns, boats, and kids' market; Itinerary 6, with the Morning of the Future's Science World made just for kids. For child care, contact Baby Sitter Next Door, tel: 604 261 8482.

USEFUL ADDRESSES

Consulates

Australia	604 684 1177
France	604 681 4345
Germany	604 684 8377
Great Britain	604 683 4421
Ireland	604 683 9233
Japan	604 684 5868
Mexico	604 684 3547
Netherlands	604 684 6448
New Zealand	604 684 7388
United States	604 685 4311

Visitor Attractions

UBC Museum of Anthropology
6393 NW Marine Drive, tel: 822 5087 (summer: daily, 10am-5pm, Tues until 9pm; winter: Tues 11am–9pm, Wed–Sun 11am–5pm;

Top: walk this way

practical information

closed Mon). First Nations Pacific Northwest culture (see Itinerary 3).

Vancouver Art Gallery
750 Hornby Street at Robson, tel: 604 662 4700 (daily 10am–5.30pm, Thur until 9pm; closed Mon Oct–April). Canadian artist Emily Carr and regular visiting exhibitions (see Itinerary 1).

Vancouver Lookout!
Harbour Centre Tower, 555 West Hastings Street, between Seymour and Richards, tel: 604 689 0421; www.vancouverlookout.com. A glass elevator takes visitors to a 360-degree birds-eye viewing area in the heart of the city.

Lynn Canyon Park and Suspension Bridge
3663 Park Road, North Vancouver, tel: 604 981 3103. A beautiful forest park and canyon with a rushing stream spanned by a 72-m (240-ft) suspension bridge.

Grouse Mountain Skyride
Capilano Road, North Vancouver, tel: 604 984 0661. A 12-minute aerial tram ride to the top of Grouse Mountain, with hikes and other attractions *(see Itinerary 10)*.

Reifel Migratory Bird Sanctuary
Highway 17 turn-off from 99 south, tel: 604 946 6980 (daily 9am–4pm). Thousands of migratory birds visit this reserve in the wetlands of the Fraser River estuary.

Walk the Dykes
Pitt Meadows, tel: 604 460 8300. Travel north on Harris Road to the gravel car park, to enjoy up to 50km (30 miles) of scenic (Dutch-made) dykes along the Alouette River, with eagles, waterfowl and lovely rural farmlands.

FURTHER READING

Insight Guide: Vancouver & Surroundings (Insight Guides, London, 2005). Comprehensive and readable guide to the city and region illustrated with excellent photographs.
Easy Hiking Around Vancouver: An All-Season Guide by Jean Cousins and Heather Robinson (Douglas and McIntyre, 1997).
Vancouver, A City Album edited by Anne Kloppenborg et al (Douglas and McIntyre, Vancouver, 1991). An historical photo album with excerpts from the archives and press of the day.

Vancouver and Its Region edited by Graeme Wynn and Timothy Oke (UBC Press, Vancouver, 1992). Essays on the physical and socio-economic evolution of Vancouver.
Vancouver, a Visual History by Bruce MacDonald (Talon Books, Vancouver, 1992). If there's one book that every city should have and every visitor should buy, it's this one. A decade by decade, map by map history of the city.
Green Spaces of Vancouver by Anne Templeman-Klut (Brighouse Press, Vancouver, 1990). Information on hiking routes.
Legends of Vancouver by E Pauline Johnson (Douglas and McIntyre, 1998).
Looking at Indian Art of the Northwest Coast by Hilary Stewart (University of Washington Press, 1979). Classic interpretive guide to First Nations art.
Vancouver by Pat Kramer (Altitude Superguide, 1999).
The Greater Vancouver Book by Chuck Davis (Whitecap Books, 1998). Almost everything you ever wanted to know about Vancouver.
Vancouver: Secrets of the City by Shawn Blore (*Vancouver* Magazine, Arsenal Pulp, 1999). Strange, but true: facts compiled by the editors of *Vancouver* Magazine.
109 Walks in British Columbia's Lower Mainland by Mary and David Macaree. (Douglas and McIntyre, 1997). A guide to walks through stunning BC.
Where to See Wildlife on Vancouver Island by Kim Goldberg (Harbour Publishing, 1997). Fifty hotspots for wildlife viewing in Vancouver, British Columbia.

Right: having a whale of a time

ACKNOWLEDGEMENTS

Photography

1, 5, 6T/B, 7T/B, 8/9, 16, 21, 23T/B, 29B, 31, 34, 36, 38, 40B, 41, 44, 45, 46, 47, 48, 49, 52, 53, 55, 56, 57T/B, 61T, 63T/B, 64, 65, 71, 72, 74, 76, 81, 83, 87, 90, 91	**Joel W Rogers**
2/3, 11, 20, 24, 25, 26, 27, 29T, 30, 32, 33, 35, 37, 39, 40T, 42, 43, 50, 51, 54, 60, 61B, 62, 66, 68, 75, 78, 82, 84, 85, 86, 89	**Richard Nowitz**
12, 13T, 14, 15	**Stanley Young/Vancouver Public Library**
13B	**City of Vancouver Archives**
10	**Bob Rowan/Corbis**
58, 59	**Kevin R. Morris/Corbis**
Front cover	**Geostock/Getty Images**
Back cover bottom	**Richard Nowitz**
Back cover top	**Joel W Rogers**

Map Production Mapping Ideas Ltd

© 2006 Apa Publications GmbH & Co. Verlag KG Singapore Branch, Singapore

Cartography Zoë Goodwin
Cover Design Klaus Geisler
Production Linton Donaldson

INDEX

index